WHAT THE **BIBLE** TEACHES ABOUT

THE TRINITY

WHAT THE **BIBLE** TEACHES ABOUT

THE TRINITY

Stuart Olyott

PUBLISHING WITH A MISSION

EP BOOKS
Faverdale North, Darlington, DL3 0PH, England

web: http://www.epbooks.org
e-mail: sales@epbooks.org

EP BOOKS USA
P. O. Box 614, Carlisle, PA 17013, USA

web: http://www.epbooks.us
e-mail: usasales@epbooks.org

First published 1979, under the title *The Three are one*.
This edition 2011.

British Library Cataloguing in Publication Data available

ISBN 13: 978-0-85234-746-1
ISBN 10: 0-85234-746-4

Printed and bound in the UK by Charlesworth, Wakefield, West Yorkshire.

I wish to thank the triune God for my father and mother

STANLEY and EILEEN OLYOTT.

They love the Lord.

Contents

Introduction

For as long as I can remember I have been able to read. In other words, I do not remember learning. I imagine that I started with some sort of *primer*, from which I learned the alphabet and simple words. My debt to that book can never be calculated, for it was the foundation for all my future reading. And yet I do not remember anything about it.

This short book is also a primer, and I hope that from it you will go on to read further. It is not a book to tell you all that you need to know. It is intended simply *to help you make a start*. It introduces you to the most basic teaching concerning the Trinity. It will remove that sense of strangeness that you may feel as you first approach this deep subject and make it possible for you to progress where once you thought you would never begin.

May we all spend our lives as those who 'pursue the knowledge of the LORD' (Hosea 6:3)!

1.
My God, how wonderful you are!

This book must begin by declaring that *God is*. This is not something that can be proved, nor does it need to be. Every man and woman knows it to be true. Man has a sense of God built into him. It is something that he knows in his heart — something left over from the time when mankind was in touch with God, and obeyed his law. Man still has a sense of this law, which is seen in his sense of right and wrong. There cannot be a sense of law unless there is a Lawgiver. Added to this, there is the sky above, and the creation around, both of which speak of God's everlasting power and deity. When a person says, 'There is no God,' he is being deliberately ignorant of a fact which he knows to be true.

But we can know much more about God than this, if we turn to the Bible. Here God has revealed to the human race all that we need to know about him, and all that he requires of us. All the books of the Bible owe their origin to him. The human writers were 'borne along' by the Holy Spirit in such a way that they produced exactly what God planned. The words they wrote are the words he intended. And yet this happened without any interference with their natural talents, and without any stereotyping of their personalities. The Bible is not the word of men, but the Word of God. This means that we do not have to sit and wonder what God is like. We do not have to guess. He has told us himself.

A Spirit

He tells us that he is a Spirit (John 4:24). He does not have a body, as we do. He is invisible — no one has ever seen him, or can see him (1 Timothy 6:15-16). He cannot be felt with the senses, or weighed, or measured. It is true that we sometimes read of his eyes, his ears, his mouth, and so on. But this is just a way of making clear to our poor minds that God sees all things, hears his people's prayers and makes himself known. God cannot be pictured or represented in any way, and he forbids us to try to depict him (Exodus 20:4).

However, we must be careful to remember that God is a personal Spirit. In other words, we must not think of him as a *Something* which we cannot describe, but as a *Someone*. He has names, the best known of which is 'Jehovah'. This is simply an English version of the Hebrew name 'Yahweh', and in our Bibles this is usually translated 'the LORD'. He has communication with men and women, and more than one has become known as his 'friend' (Exodus 33:11; James 2:23). On the very first page of our Bible we read of him speaking, and this continues all the way to the last page. We learn again and again that it is possible to *know* God. This would not be possible if he were just a force or an influence which we could never describe.

Very great

Because God is a Spirit, he is not limited in any way, and there is no person or thing which may be likened or compared to him (Isaiah 40:18).

So far as space is concerned, he is everywhere (1 Kings 8:27; Psalm 139:7-10). '"Do I not fill heaven and earth?" says the LORD' (Jeremiah 23:24). He is in all places at all times, and there is no place from which he is absent. We must not think that only *part* of God is to be found in any particular place in the universe. The *whole* of God is present there. He is there in all his majesty and glory and the totality of his being. And this is true of all places, all the time. How can this be? Our mortal minds cannot take it in. The finite cannot understand the infinite! All we can do is believe what God has declared concerning himself, and bow in adoring wonder.

> All we can do is believe what God has declared concerning himself, and bow in adoring wonder.

So far as time is concerned, he is eternal (Isaiah 40:28; Habakkuk 1:12). 'Even from everlasting to everlasting,

You are God' (Psalm 90:2). He alone has immortality in and of himself (1 Timothy 6:16). He inhabits eternity, and his years have no end (Isaiah 57:15; Hebrews 1:11-12). This, too, is beyond our comprehension. Everything owes its beginning to him, but he himself had no beginning. He is; he always has been; he always will be. This is what is meant by the quaint expression 'world without end', which is often used in some church services. There is no change in him: there never has been, and there never will be, for he is always the same (Malachi 3:6; James 1:17). All things depend on him, but his own existence does not depend on anything or anyone other than himself. He is the Fountain of his own being. This is why one of his names is 'the living God' (Revelation 7:2). This is also why he announced his name to Moses as 'I AM WHO I AM' (Exodus 3:14).

So far as knowledge is concerned, he knows everything (Psalm 139:2-5; 1 John 3:20). 'His understanding is infinite' (Psalm 147:5). For ourselves, we have to learn one thing at a time, and our knowledge is always small. There is no such thing as learning so far as God is concerned. He knows all things as they really are, all at once. There is no limit to his understanding. It is a mystery to us how this can be so. But nothing is a mystery to God. There is nothing which he does not fully understand. There is nothing of which he is ignorant or uncertain and, of course, this means that he cannot be deceived.

So far as power is concerned, he does whatever he chooses (Psalm 135:6; Daniel 4:35). 'He does whatever He pleases' (Psalm 115:3). What he pleases to do is decided by his own nature. Because he is holy, he cannot ever choose to depart from what is pure and right. Because he is perfect in every way, he cannot ever choose to change. A change would be either for better or for worse. If for better, it would show that he was not already perfect; if for worse, he would become less than perfect. It is true that he sometimes chooses to change the way in which he deals with a man or a woman, but this is because there has been a change in the person concerned, and not because there is ever any change in him. Nothing that he chooses to do ever fails to happen (Isaiah 46:10). Because he is God alone, and all other beings are his creatures, his will can never be resisted (Romans 9:19; Daniel 4:35). Everything in the universe, however small, serves his purposes. It brings to pass what he has planned and decided (Ephesians 1:11).

Unique

What we have read so far tells us what God is in himself. But it is not enough to say that he is a personal Spirit, who is everywhere, eternal, all-knowing and all-powerful. What is this God *like*? What sort of God is he?

He is *holy*. 'God is light and in Him is no darkness at all' (1 John 1:5). His character is perfect. He is pure and entirely free from wicked and dishonest motives, thoughts, words and actions. But it is hard to explain precisely what holiness is. The heavenly creatures which surround God's throne are totally free from all impurity, and yet they cannot look on the majesty of God, and call to one another in perpetual amazement, 'Holy, holy, holy is the LORD of hosts…' (Isaiah 6:3). No wonder that

15

God is described as 'glorious in holiness' (Exodus 15:11)! It is this characteristic which cuts him off, and marks him out as quite different from all his creatures (Psalm 99:3; Isaiah 40:25). How can a man approach such a God (Psalm 24:3)? He is of purer eyes than to behold evil, and cannot look on wickedness (Habakkuk 1:13).

He is *righteous*. 'The LORD is righteous in all His ways' (Psalm 145:17), and this never alters (Zephaniah 3:5). His rule of his creation is firmly founded on the twin pillars of righteousness and justice (Psalm 97:2). He always does what is right. Every sentence he gives is justified, and he can never be blamed for any judgement that he makes, for he is inflexibly just (Genesis 18:25; Psalm 51:4). How comforting that it is he, and he alone, who will judge the world! The last judgement will be fair. No mistakes will be made. Nobody will receive from God either more or less than he deserved (Psalm 96:13).

He is *loving*. 'God is love' (1 John 4:8, 16). He is 'the LORD, the LORD God, merciful and gracious, longsuffering, and abounding in goodness and truth' (Exodus 34:6); a God of 'lovingkindness' and 'tender mercies' (Psalm 51:1); 'slow to anger, and of great kindness' (Joel 2:13; Jonah 4:2); who 'delights in mercy' (Micah 7:18). How marvellous! The holy God, who is inflexibly just, is love! His justice demanded my punishment, and it was satisfied when the innocent Substitute died in my place (1 Peter 3:18). His love planned my salvation, and that is why he sent the Saviour to die (1 John 4:10). Love and justice are not opposites. Both are found in God, and both are found in his action at the cross.

He is *good*. 'The LORD is good to all' (Psalm 145:9). 'You are good, and do good' (Psalm 119:68). By nature men and women prefer not to have God in their thoughts, and choose to go their own way. They are opposed to the idea that he should rule their lives, and would rather choose their own objects of worship. Yet every day God is actively good to such people who are, in fact, his enemies. 'He did not leave Himself without witness, in that He did good, gave us rain from heaven and fruitful seasons, filling our hearts with food and gladness' (Acts 14:17). The ripening of the harvest, the sustenance of the animals, and every other good thing which this universe enjoys, come from him (Psalm 85:12; 104:24-31; James 1:17). But the greatest evidence of his goodness is seen in his treatment of those of his enemies who forsake their hateful attitude, and turn to him for pardon. 'For You, Lord, are good, and ready to forgive, and abundant in mercy to all those who call upon You' (Psalm 86:5).

He is *wise*. 'Blessed be the name of God for ever and ever, for wisdom and might are His' (Daniel 2:20). When we see the beauty and harmony of his creation, and the intricacy of the design of the smallest creature, we are compelled to say, 'O LORD, how manifold are Your works! In wisdom You have made them all. The earth is full of Your possessions' (Psalm 104:24). The skills which men exercise and develop, the very existence of knowledge and understanding in our race, the way that all that takes place brings God's purposes to pass — all these things are due to the wisdom of God (Isaiah 28:23-29; 31:2; Daniel 2:21). His wisdom and understanding are infinite, and totally beyond our power to investigate and understand.

'Oh, the depth of the riches both of the wisdom and knowledge of God! How unsearchable are His judgements and His ways past finding out! "For who has known the mind of the LORD? Or who has become His counsellor?" "Or who has first given to Him and it shall be repaid to him?" For of Him and through Him and to Him are all things, to whom be glory for ever. Amen' (Romans 11:33-36).

Incomprehensible

So we see that what God says about himself is clear enough. But it is all too wonderful for the human mind to grasp. We cannot take it in, for his thoughts and ways are so much higher than ours (Isaiah 55:8-9). We can see *what* the truth is, but we cannot explain *how* it can be so. Our minds are too limited. Only God understands God. Can any man or woman explain how it is possible for God to exist as a personal Being, without a body? Can we grasp how all of God can be in all places at all times? Do we really understand the concept that he had no beginning, and is without change of any sort? Is it not true that our minds are baffled when we try to think of what it means to be all-knowing? How can he do all that he pleases without being selfish? How can he be perfectly holy, righteous, loving, good and wise, all at the same time?

No question about God which contains the word 'how' can be answered. Our mortal minds are too poor for that. But questions which contain the word 'what' can be answered plainly and clearly, because God has revealed the answers in the Scriptures. We are able to study, and we are able to state what God has said. We are able to say what the truth is. But we are not able to explain how it can be so. We are overwhelmed by what we learn. The more we consider it, the more we realize that there is no appropriate reaction to what we read, except to become a reverent worshipper.

> No question about God which contains the word 'how' can be answered. Our mortal minds are too poor for that.

The truth of the Trinity, which we are about to examine, is a greater mystery than anything else that can be said about God. We will never understand how God, who is one, is three. But we do not come to the subject asking, 'How can these things be?' We come as humble learners, searching the Scriptures, and asking, 'What has God said?' We rejoice that he has told us so much about himself, and trust his perfect wisdom which has decided to reveal nothing more. We are humbled that we cannot enter anywhere, except where he has permitted. We are not as God. We are creatures. We can never discover what he has not revealed. We can never understand what he has not explained. But,

> Where reason fails, with all her powers,
> There faith prevails and love adores.

2.
God is one

Only one God

'How many Gods are there?'
'One,' replied the little boy.

'How do you know that?'

'Because there is only room for one, for he fills heaven and earth.'

No truth is more plainly taught in Scripture than this. There is but one God who really exists.

If this were not so, we would have to assume that there are more gods than one. This is something which Scripture constantly denies. There are no other gods at all. Mankind at large does not believe this to be so, and there have been, and are, false gods without number. But none of these is a true god. None of these is the living God.

It is true that the word 'god' is sometimes used of angels (Psalm 97:7). This is because they are spiritual creatures of high rank and excellence. The title is also used of rulers and judges (Psalm 82:1, 6), because of their authority over others. Satan, the devil, is called 'the god of this age' (2 Corinthians 4:4) because of the dominion over the wicked which he has wrongfully seized. But these are all figurative uses of the word 'god'. Scripture continues to insist that there is but one true God, one living God.

So it was that from his earliest years a little Jewish boy was taught to recite the words of Deuteronomy 6:4: 'Hear, O Israel: The LORD our God, the LORD is one!' It was the most basic belief of the Jewish faith, built, as it was, on the Old Testament. It was a belief from which no Jew could be shifted. He knew that 'the LORD Himself is God; there is none other besides Him' (Deuteronomy 4:35).

The Jew would think back to the time when the glorious temple of Solomon was dedicated. After praying urgently and at length to God, the king turned to the people, and expressed his most heartfelt desire: 'May the LORD our God be with us, as He was with our fathers. May He not leave us nor forsake us … that all the peoples of the earth may know that the LORD is God; there is no other' (1 Kings 8:57, 60). That expressed perfectly what every Jew felt. He was to be a witness to an ignorant world that there is no other God but the Lord.

He would think back to the days of the great prophet Isaiah, and the words which God spoke to him: 'Thus says the LORD, the King of Israel, and his Redeemer, the LORD of hosts: "I am the First and I am the Last; besides Me there is no God"' (Isaiah 44:6). The God who spoke these words announced himself as the King of Israel. The Jew saw it as his great mission to uphold the truth that there is no other God but Jehovah. How he loved to read, 'I am the LORD, and there is no other; there is no God besides Me ... I am the LORD, and there is no other' (Isaiah 45:5-6)!

Jesus himself was reared to know and love the Old Testament Scriptures, and consistently maintained their truth. The confession of the uniqueness of God was something he unreservedly took upon his own lips (Mark 12:29, 32), and it was also taught quite clearly by his apostles (1 Corinthians 8:4-6; Ephesians 4:6; James 2:19). It is the clear declaration of the whole Scripture.

God is one

The Old Testament was written in Hebrew, and when the Jew recited Deuteronomy 6:4, he did it in that language — as he still does today. Unfortunately our English language cannot perfectly translate in one sentence precisely what Deuteronomy 6:4 means. It means more than 'The LORD our God, the LORD is one!' That can be taken simply as a statement that there is no other God but the LORD. He is the *only* one. It can also be translated, 'The LORD our God, the LORD is one.' He is not just the only one. He who is the only one, is *one*.

What are we trying to say here? 'God is one in His essential being or constitutional nature,' writes Louis Berkhof. But what does *that* mean? It means that God cannot be divided or split up. You cannot have a collection of pieces which are less than God, put them together, and have *God*! He is not like a jigsaw.

Nor is he like a human body, made up of many organs. You cannot add eternity and unchangeability and all-power and holiness together, and make up God. He is not made up of parts. He is indivisible. He is one. All of him is eternal. All of him is unchangeable. All of him is all-powerful. All of him is holy. You cannot, for instance, take away his holiness, and leave most of God behind. If you *could* take away his holiness you would have destroyed God, for *all* that he is is holy.

This is what theologians mean when they talk about God being 'one indivisible essence'. The word 'essence' or 'being' can be used almost interchangeably with the word 'substance'. This does not mean that God is *made* of anything. Later in the book we shall talk of the Father and the Son and the Holy Spirit being of 'the same substance'. We shall not mean that they are composed of the same 'stuff'. We shall mean that although they are distinct, they are the same one God. All that God is is the Father. All that God is is the Son. All that God is is the Holy Spirit. Each one is all that God is. Each one is God in the same sense — of the same essence, being or substance. And yet God is indivisible.

> All that God is is the Father. All that God is is the Son. All that God is is the Holy Spirit. Each one is all that God is.

Let us put it another way, to stress what we are saying. The Father is Jehovah. The Son is Jehovah. The Holy Spirit is Jehovah. But we must never think that there are three Jehovahs. It is here that the mystery lies, and we are running ahead of ourselves. For the moment we must be content to know that there is only one Jehovah, and that the Jehovah, who is, is *one*.

More than one who is God

And yet even at this stage it needs to be said that from the earliest times it has been clear that there is more than one who is Jehovah. Notice what we are saying. There is not more than one God. We have just seen that. Yet there is more than one who *is* God. There is a single God. And yet there is a plurality of Persons in the divine essence.

You can see this on almost the first page of your Bible. Genesis 1:26-27 reads: 'Then God said, "Let *Us* make man in *Our* image, according to *Our* likeness … So God created man in *His* own image.' The words I have put in italics show that God, who is one, speaks as more than one. The verses emphasize both the unity and the plurality of God. Two or three pages later on we read, 'Then the LORD God said, "Behold, the man has become like one of *Us*…"' (Genesis 3:22); and in chapter 11:5-7 we read, 'But the LORD came down … And the LORD said … let *Us* go down…' Only one God is to be found in all these passages. And yet he speaks in the plural! There is more than one who is God. So it was that centuries later Isaiah heard Jehovah saying, 'Whom shall *I* send, and who will go for *Us*?' (Isaiah 6:8).

Just as extraordinary are those Old Testament passages which refer to 'the Angel of the LORD'. It is quite plain that this person is God himself. It is equally plain that he is to be distinguished from God. The word 'angel' means 'messenger' or 'one sent', and the phrase 'the Angel of the LORD' therefore means 'the one sent by Jehovah'. Genesis 16:7-13 records how Hagar, who had run away from Abram and Sarai, was commanded by 'the Angel of the LORD' to return. It is then made clear that it was the Lord himself who was speaking to her, and she called the place where she met him 'the well of the One who lives and sees me'. The one who was sent by God was God himself!

Abraham himself had a visit from the Angel of the Lord some time later, in the plains of Mamre (Genesis 18). The visitor appeared as a man (v. 2), but it is clearly stated that it was the Lord himself (vv. 1, 13-14). Abraham recognized this, and offered prayer to him (vv. 23-33).

This was not the last time that Abraham was to meet the Angel of the Lord. It was none other than the Angel who stopped him from slaying his son Isaac (Genesis 22:11, 15). Abraham called the name of the place, 'The Lord will provide' (v. 14), for once more he clearly recognized the identity of the heavenly Visitor. The Angel gave him a promise, which began: 'By Myself I have sworn, says the Lord…' (v. 16). The one whom the Lord sent *was* the Lord!

There are many references to the Angel in the Old Testament, and on each occasion it is plain that God's messenger *is* God. It is 'the Angel of the Lord' who speaks to Moses from the burning bush, and says, 'I am the God of your father…' (Exodus 3:6), and goes on to reveal his name as 'I AM WHO I AM' (v. 14). That Angel is the God who led Jacob and redeemed him (Genesis 48:15-16), and is the Lord himself who goes ahead of the Israelites as they flee from Egypt (Exodus 13:21; 14:19). It is the Angel of the Lord who appears twice in the book of Judges, and on each occasion reveals that he is God himself (Judges 6:11-12, 14, 16; 13:3, 9, 22). So we have God sent by God!

The prophecy of Isaiah revealed something similar. He told Israel that the Lord God would give a sign, which would be a son born of a virgin. His name would be Immanuel, which means 'God with us' (Isaiah 7:14). This one whom God would send would himself be 'Mighty God' (Isaiah 9:6). How could God send God if there was not more than one person who was God? And yet we must not forget the verses from Isaiah which we mentioned earlier. The same book insists that there is no God except the one whom Israel worshipped. One God; yet more than one who *is* God.

So it is that the Old Testament tells us of God anointing God (Psalm 45:6-7); the LORD God and his Spirit sending one who is himself God (Isaiah 48:16-17); and Jehovah raising up a promised King who will be Jehovah (Jeremiah 23:5-6)! Again and again we are confronted by the mysterious truth that the one God is more than one.

We are not saying that the doctrine of the Trinity was completely revealed in the Old Testament; but nor are we saying that it was completely absent. The Old Testament believer knew that there was a plurality in the Godhead. Indeed, he even had some faint indications that the one God is three. When the priest blessed the Israelites, and put God's name upon them, did he not always use the name of Jehovah three times (Numbers 6:22-27)? Had not Isaiah overheard the seraphim acknowledge the Lord as three times holy (Isaiah 6:3)? All this was a preparation for the truth which the New Testament was to unveil fully. The God revealing himself little by

> The God revealing himself little by little in Old Testament days at last sent his Son into the world, and later took up his abode in believers' hearts by his Holy Spirit.

little in Old Testament days at last sent his Son into the world, and later took up his abode in believers' hearts by his Holy Spirit. The doctrine of the Trinity was not revealed as a series of sentences or propositions. It was God's work of salvation which finally made it clear. The Christian believer can read the Old Testament, and understand it much more easily than the original readers. The passages which speak of God as one, and yet more than one, make good sense to him. He does not stumble over the verses which speak both of God's unity and his plurality. He is not surprised to read of God having a discussion with himself, or to survey the promises that God would send God into the world. He still cannot grasp how God can be One-in-Three and Three-in-One. Yet he knows that it *is* so. The Old Testament believer had many clues, but never saw the truth as clearly as that. What was dark to him is light to us.

3.
The Father is God

We are only just beginning chapter 3, and yet I must, at once, say something about chapter 4. In chapter 4 we shall see that the Lord Jesus Christ is God. Yet when he taught his disciples to pray to God, he did not invite them to pray to *him*. He said, 'In this manner, therefore, pray: Our Father...' (Matthew 6:9).

Prayer to God is not to be addressed to the Lord Jesus Christ, but to one who is distinct from him — the Father! There is one who is God, who is not the Lord Jesus Christ, and who goes by the name of 'Father'. But before we pursue this, we ought to notice that the Scriptures do not always use the name 'Father' in the same way.

The Father of all

Sometimes, for instance, 'Father' is used, not of one who is distinct from the Son and the Holy Spirit — a distinct person in the Godhead — but of the Godhead himself.

Let us give some examples of this. When Paul is writing to the Christians at Corinth, he reminds them that the idols who surround them are not real gods at all. This is not what their worshippers think, but it is the truth. The idols do not represent deities who have a real existence. There is only one God who has a real existence, and it is the one that Christians worship. So he writes, 'Yet for us there is one God, the Father' (1 Corinthians 8:6). Here the word 'Father' equals the words 'one God'. Paul is saying that there is but one God, and is not thinking of the persons of the Godhead at all. It is in this sense that he uses the word 'Father', just as he does in Ephesians 4:6, where he writes of 'one God and Father of all'.

The writer to the Hebrews does something similar in chapter 12 verse 9. Here he explains that God treats Christian believers as his children. Just as a father chastises only his own children, so God brings unpleasant experiences into the lives of believers, in order to develop their characters. These experiences are not something to resent, but to accept. They should not decrease our regard for God, but should rather increase it. 'We have had human fathers who corrected us, and we paid them respect. Shall we not much more readily be in subjection to the Father of spirits and live?' Once more the title 'Father' is used of God, but not of a distinct person in the Godhead. This is exactly how James uses it when he writes, 'Every good gift and every perfect gift is from above, and comes down from the Father of lights...' (James 1:17).

The Father of Israel

The name 'Father' is also used to express the fact that the Old Testament people of Israel had God as their Ruler and Head. 'The LORD… Is He not your Father, who bought you?' (Deuteronomy 32:6). 'Father' is here simply an alternative word for God, without any thought of distinct persons in the Godhead. So Isaiah prayed, 'You, O LORD, are our Father; our Redeemer…'; 'But now, O LORD, You are our Father; we are the clay, and You our potter; and all we are the work of Your hand' (Isaiah 63:16; 64:8).

Not all members of Old Testament Israel had such confidence in God. So in the days of Jeremiah, God says to them through the prophet, 'Will you not from this time cry to Me, "My Father, You are the guide of my youth"?' (Jeremiah 3:4). In later times every Israelite spoke of God as the nation's Father. But he did not necessarily acknowledge this in practice. God was not given the honour due to him, and the individual Israelites did not treat each other as brothers. This time the rebuke was: 'If then I am the Father, where is My honour?…'; 'Have we not all one Father? Has not one God created us? Why do we deal treacherously with one another…?' (Malachi 1:6; 2:10).

The Father of believers

So by the time the Lord Jesus Christ came, the Jews were used to using the name 'Father' as a substitute for the word 'God'. They taught that they, and they alone, stood in relation to God as children do to their father. This was an idea which

Christ and his apostles had to correct. All men are certainly not the children of God. But nor are all Jews: this is a privilege which belongs exclusively to those who repent and believe the gospel. Only they enjoy intimacy with God, and the comfort of his tender care. Such people, and not the Jews, are the true Israel which God recognizes. They alone are therefore entitled to address God as 'Father'.

It was to his disciples only that Jesus ever spoke of 'your Father in heaven' (Matthew 5:45). It was to them alone that he spoke of 'your Father ... your Father ... your heavenly Father' (Matthew 6:6, 8, 14). 'We are children of God' (Romans 8:16) was written only of those who are right with God by means of faith in the Lord Jesus Christ. Adoption into God's family, and having him as their Father, is their highest privilege. And it is theirs alone. It is shared by nobody else whatever. They, and they alone, can exultingly rejoice, saying, 'Behold what manner of love the Father has bestowed on us, that we should be called children of God!' (1 John 3:1).

The Father of the Lord Jesus Christ

Now the Lord Jesus Christ is God, as we shall shortly see. But although Christians have God as their Father, it is *not* the Lord Jesus Christ who is that Father. God the Father is someone distinct from him. The Father of believers is also the Father of Christ, though in a different sense. Christian believers are his adopted children, while Christ is his eternal Son. Why did Jesus say to Mary, 'I am ascending to My Father and your Father'? (John 20:17). Why did he not say, 'I am ascending to *our* Father'? His words show us that God is Father of us both. But the words are put as they are to emphasize that God is a Father to Christ in a way that he is *not* Father to us.

It is in John's Gospel that we see most clearly that although the Father is God, and the Lord Jesus Christ is God, they are, none the less, distinct. Within the being of God, one is the Father of the other, and one is the Son of the other. Almost at the beginning of the Gospel we read, 'And the Word became flesh and dwelt among us, and we beheld His glory, the glory as of the only begotten of the Father, full of grace and truth' (John 1:14). This tells us that the Word, who is the Lord Jesus Christ, is quite distinct from God the Father. One became flesh, and the other did not. And yet the glory of Christ is the glory of the Father, so they must obviously be God in the same sense. Christ is the perfect expression of the Father — which is what John meant when he described him as 'the Word'.

Almost at once we read, 'No one has seen God at any time. The only begotten Son, who is in the bosom of the Father, He has declared Him' (John 1:18). But we know from our previous chapter that there are people who *have* seen God! What the verse must mean is that nobody has seen God the Father. Whenever people have seen God, it is the Lord Jesus Christ, the Son, that they have seen. That is who 'the Angel of the LORD' was. The Son is quite distinct from the Father, which is why he is described as 'in the bosom of the Father'. And yet to see him is to see God,

> Christ is the perfect expression of the Father — which is what John meant when he described him as 'the Word'.

for he expresses and declares God perfectly. Both are God. But one is not the other. Yet there remains but one true and living God. We must not think we have missed out in any way, because we have not seen God the Father. Jesus stands before the world and announces, 'I and My Father are one' (John 10:30); 'And he who sees Me sees Him who sent Me' (John 12:45); 'He who has seen Me has seen the Father; so how can you say, "Show us the Father"?' (John 14:9).

When Jesus spoke in such intimate terms about God the Father, the Jews plotted to kill him (John 5:17-31). No one disputed the fact that the Father was God. It had never been questioned. But Jesus' language clearly implied that he was making himself equal with the Father — equal with God. They knew that there was only one God, and that the Father was that God. Despite the Old Testament clues which we have examined, they could not conceive that more than one could be God. The whole idea of a plurality in the Godhead escaped them. It seemed clear to them that Jesus was asserting himself to be equal with God. They took this to mean that he claimed to be an *additional* God. To them this was blasphemy, and this explains why they wanted to kill him. They held so fiercely to the deity of the Father, that they could not conceive of the deity of another (John 8:53-59). They were wrong about the second, as we shall now see. But they were not wrong about the first. The Father *is* God.

4.
The Lord Jesus Christ, the Son, is God

The Scriptures are full of evidence that Jesus Christ is God. It is a truth that no one need doubt.

Pre-existence

Of all the men and women who have walked this earth, only of Jesus Christ can it be said that his life did not begin when he was born. He existed before that time. He was in the beginning, and all things were made by him (John 1:1-3; Colossians 1:15-18). He was rich before he became poor (2 Corinthians 8:9). 'I came forth from the Father', he said, 'and have come into the world' (John 16:28). He described himself as 'He who came down from heaven' (John 3:13), and asked his hearers what they would think if they saw him 'ascend where He was before' (John 6:62).

He clearly meant us to understand that he is God, who has come among us as a Man. What else could he have meant when he prayed in the presence of his disciples, 'And now, O Father, glorify Me together with Yourself, with the glory which I had with You before the world was' (John 17:5)? His claims to be God were well understood by the Jews, for they took up stones to stone him when they heard him say, 'Before Abraham was, I AM' (John 8:58). If he had said, 'Before Abraham was, I *was*', it would not have been so bad. They could have been charitable, and written him off as some kind of crank. But he did not say that. He said, 'I AM.' He was claiming a continued ever-present existence from before Abraham's time to that moment. And had not God described himself as 'I AM'? What else could Jesus be doing, but laying claim to deity? The Jews did not believe the claim, but considered it a blasphemy — and took up stones...

Names and titles

Before Jesus began his public ministry, there had taken place the preaching of John the Baptist. He announced that he had come in fulfilment of the prophecy of Isaiah 40:3: 'The voice of one crying in the wilderness: "Prepare the way of the LORD; make straight in the desert a highway for our God."'

In the East, a forerunner often went ahead of a very important person. It was his job to smooth the road, so that the dignitary who was following did not have too bumpy a ride!

John the Baptist made it clear that the one following him was Jehovah himself. He was God (John 1:23). He underlined this by saying, 'He who comes after me ranks higher than I do, for he existed before me' (John 1:15, my own translation). When Jesus eventually came to Jordan, John positively identified him as the one of whom he had been speaking (John 1:29-30). Jesus is the promised Jehovah! Jesus is God! Yet John's titles for the promised one were 'Lamb of God', and 'Son of God' (John 1:29, 34). The Son of God is God. But the Son is not the Father, for as John baptized Jesus, a voice sounded from heaven, declaring, 'You are My beloved Son; in You I am well pleased' (Luke 3:22).

The Jews well understood that the title 'Son of God' was a title for one who was fully God. When Jesus stood trial the night before his crucifixion, the high priest asked him: 'I put You under oath by the living God: Tell us if You are the Christ, the Son of God!' (Matthew 26:63). Jesus admitted this to be true. Matthew tells us what follows: 'Then the high priest tore his clothes, saying, "He has spoken blasphemy! What further need do we have of witnesses? Look, now you have heard His blasphemy!"' (Matthew 26:65). He was convinced that Jesus had spoken blasphemy, because he understood perfectly that the title 'Son of God' is a divine title. Of course, it was not blasphemy but the truth. The high priest and the Jewish council did not believe it.

But the disciples did! The glorious truth of Christ's real identity had flashed into their minds a year or two earlier. Speaking for them all, Peter had said to Jesus, 'You are the Christ, the Son of the living God' (Matthew 16:16); 'You have the words of eternal life. Also we have come to believe and know that You are the Christ, the Son of the living God' (John 6:68-69). In the same way, when Paul became a Christian believer, 'Immediately he preached the Christ in the synagogues, that He is the Son of God' (Acts 9:20). He rejoiced to recall that Jesus was God's 'own Son' (Romans 8:3).

It was the same with John. He tells us that the glory he saw in Jesus' life was the glory of the Father's only Son (John 1:14). He was with the Father at the beginning (1 John 1:1-2). He is 'the Word' who was 'in the beginning with God' (John 1:1-2). Not only was he *with* God, but 'the Word *was* God' (John 1:1). John is as dogmatic as that about the deity of Christ. The glory of Jehovah which Isaiah witnessed about 700 B.C. was none other than the glory of Christ (Isaiah 6; John 12:39-41). The very aim which John had in writing his Gospel was to persuade us that 'Jesus is the Christ, the Son of God' (John 20:31).

The Son of God is God himself. The word 'LORD' which is so often used of him also serves to make this clear. When the Old Testament was eventually translated into Greek, *kyrios* was the word which was used to translate 'Jehovah'. The New Testament was written in Greek, and it is the same word *kyrios* which is translated 'LORD' in our English versions. The word used for Jehovah is the word used for the Lord Jesus Christ! We are not surprised — for Jesus is God. The writer to the Hebrews refers the words, 'Your throne, O God, is for ever and ever,' to the Lord Jesus Christ (Psalm 45:6-7; Hebrews 1:8). This is but one of many occasions where Old Testament passages which referred to Jehovah are applied to Christ by the New Testament writers. By looking at these passages we can quickly see that it is proper to speak of Christ as 'God': Numbers 21:5-6 and 1 Corinthians 10:9; 'O my God … You are the same, and Your years will have no end' (Psalm 102:24-27; Hebrews 1:10-12); 'The King, the LORD of hosts' (Isaiah 6:1-10; John 12:39-41); 'The LORD of hosts' (Isaiah 8:13-14; Romans 9:33); 'Mighty God' (Isaiah 9:1-6; Matthew 4:14-16); and 'The Lord' (Malachi 3:1; Matthew 11:10).

In the same vein, Paul is not ashamed to call him 'God … who is over all' (Romans 9:5); and 'our great God and Saviour' (Titus 2:13). He asserts his deity in such phrases as 'the grace of our God and the Lord Jesus Christ' (2 Thessalonians 1:12). The church, he tells us, was purchased by God 'with His own blood' (Acts 20:28). He goes so far as to declare that all there is of God dwells bodily in the Lord Jesus Christ. That is the full strength of the Greek words of Colossians 2:9, the verse which reads, 'For in Him dwells all the fulness of the Godhead bodily.' Whatever doubts are nursed about Jesus Christ today, it is clear who the apostles believed him to be and who they taught that he was! The Son is not the Father, but the Son is God. And he is God in the same sense as the Father is.

A man who was arguing against the deity of Christ once said, 'If it was true, it would have been stated in the clearest possible terms.' His friend replied, 'If you believed this truth, and were teaching it, what words would you choose to express it?' 'I would say,' the objector answered, 'that Jesus Christ is *the true God*.' His friend replied, 'You have hit upon the very words of Scripture. John, speaking of the Son, says, "This is *the true God* and eternal life"' (1 John 5:20).

> **The Son is not the Father, but the Son is God. And he is God in the same sense as the Father is.**

Attributes

Seeing Jesus is actually called God, we are not surprised to find that the characteristics which belong to God are ascribed to him. For instance, in Isaiah 44:6 we read of Jehovah saying, 'I am the First and I am the Last.' Yet in Revelation, Jesus says, 'I am the Alpha and the Omega, the Beginning and the End, the First and the Last' (Revelation 22:13). Jehovah is eternal; Jesus is eternal. Clearly Jesus is Jehovah: he is God.

In the same way, we know that God is unchangeable (Malachi 3:6); and yet the believer is to be comforted by knowing the Son of God as 'Jesus Christ ... the same yesterday, today, and for ever' (Hebrews 13:8). God is present everywhere, but as we go into all the world to spread the gospel, we are heartened to hear Christ's 'Lo, *I* am with you always' (Matthew 28:20). His presence everywhere is also displayed by his promise to be wherever two or three gather in his name (Matthew 18:20). God is all-powerful, but Jesus Christ 'is able even to subdue all things to Himself' (Philippians 3:21). God is all-knowing, but this, too, is so obviously true of Christ. He can read people's hearts (John 2:24-25). From the beginning he knew exactly who would betray him (John 6:70-71; 13:10-11). He predicted the details of his own death and resurrection (Matthew 16:21), and Peter's denial and restoration (Luke 22:31-34). He knows what is going on in the churches (Revelation 2:2). But the full mystery of his own person is unknowable: 'No one knows the Son except the Father' (Matthew 11:27).

'Who can forgive sins but God alone?' But Jesus authoritatively said to the paralysed man, 'Son, your sins are forgiven you' (Mark 2:7, 5); and we are urged that 'as Christ forgave you, so you also must do' (Colossians 3:13). Who but

God is holy? Yet Peter, knowing this full well, is happy to refer Psalm 16 to Christ, and to call him the 'Holy One' (Acts 2:27). We could go on with many other arguments of the same sort. In Isaiah 45:23 Jehovah pledges, 'That to Me every knee shall bow, every tongue shall take an oath.' The New Testament pledges that God will cause 'that at the name of Jesus every knee should bow … and that every tongue should confess that Jesus Christ is Lord…' (Philippians 2:10-11). Again and again we see it: what is true of Jehovah alone is true of Jesus. Jesus *is* Jehovah! What can be said of God alone is said of Christ. Christ *is* God! We need doubt no more.

> …what is true of Jehovah alone is true of Jesus. Jesus *is* Jehovah! What can be said of God alone is said of Christ.

Divine works

Who created the world? And yet of Jesus it is said, 'All things were made through Him, and without Him nothing was made that was made … the world was made through Him…'; 'For by Him all things were created … All things were created through Him and for Him' (John 1:3, 10; Colossians 1:16-17).

Who holds the universe together, and rules it? And yet of Jesus it is said, 'In Him all things consist.' He is 'upholding all things by the word of His power'. He was able to announce to his disciples, 'All authority has been given to Me in heaven and on earth' (Colossians 1:17; Hebrews 1:3; Matthew 28:18).

Who but God will raise the dead, and judge the world? Yet we read of Jesus that, '...all who are in the graves will hear His voice and come forth — those who have done good, to the resurrection of life, and those who have done evil, to the resurrection of condemnation' (John 5:28-29). 'For we must all appear before the judgement seat of Christ' (2 Corinthians 5:10). The Lord Jesus Christ claimed this most vividly in his parable of the sheep and goats. Eastern shepherds have both in their flocks, but there come times when they must separate them. He announced that he would come in his glory, and gather all nations before him: 'And He will separate them one from another, as a shepherd divides his sheep from the goats' (Matthew 25:32). Who but God could do this?

Who but God can give eternal life? But Jesus said of his people, 'And I give them eternal life' (John 10:28). Who but God can send the Holy Spirit? But Jesus promised, 'I will send Him to you' (John 16:7). Who but God can make his people holy? But Paul wrote, 'Christ also loved the church and gave Himself for her, that He might sanctify and cleanse her...' (Ephesians 5:25-26). There are things which God alone can do; but the Lord Jesus Christ does these things. He must be God.

Jesus' words and actions on this earth drive us to the same conclusion. Throughout the Old Testament we read that the prophets introduced their messages by saying, 'Thus says the Lord'. When Jesus came, his teaching, too, had a unique authority. It staggered those who heard him (Matthew 7:28-29; John 7:32, 45-46). They were accustomed to the teaching of the Jewish scribes, who spent most of their time quoting learned writers. Jesus did not speak like them; but nor did he speak like the prophets. He spoke on his *own* authority, saying, '*I* say to you' (Matthew 5:18, 20, 22, etc.). In the circumstances this was clearly a claim to deity. He spoke as God.

In the same way, he spoke to the demons, and they came out (Mark 1:21-27). His mere word was necessary — how unlike the elaborate ceremonies of the Jewish exorcists! He spoke to the wind and the sea, and they obeyed him (Mark 4:41). He spoke to the blind, and they could see; to the deaf, and they could hear (Matthew 9:27-32; Mark 7:34-35). At his word the lame walked, the diseased were healed and the dead were raised (John 5:8-9; Luke 17:11-19; Mark 5:41-42). He spoke as God, and those who witnessed his miracles sensed themselves to be in the presence of God (Luke 5:25-26; 7:16; 9:43). His miracles reveal his identity, for as John wrote, towards the end of his Gospel, 'And truly Jesus did many other signs in the presence of His disciples, which are not written in this book; but these are written that you may believe that Jesus is the Christ, the Son of God, and that believing you may have life in His name' (John 20:30-31).

Divine worship

If Jesus is God, it cannot be wrong to worship him. The Scriptures teach that worship not only *may* be given to Christ, but *should* be given to him. It is of the Lord Jesus Christ that it is commanded: 'Let all the angels of God worship Him' (Hebrews 1:6). And they do so. Countless myriads surround him in heaven, 'saying with a loud voice: "Worthy is the Lamb who was slain to receive power and riches and wisdom, and strength and honour and glory and blessing!"' (Revelation 5:12). They are joined by his people on earth, who exclaim, 'To Him who loved us and washed us from our sins in His own blood, and has made us kings and priests to His God and Father, to Him be glory and dominion for ever and ever. Amen' (Revelation 1:5-6).

It is because Christians give to Christ their worship, that they are known as those who 'call on the name of Jesus Christ our Lord' (1 Corinthians 1:2). They do this because God wills that 'all should honour the Son just as they honour the Father' (John 5:23). This is why Stephen offered prayer to Christ, in his dying moments (Acts 7:59-60). This is why converts are to be baptized in the name of the Son, as well as the Father and the Holy Spirit (Matthew 28:19). This is why, when the apostle Paul pronounced a benediction upon his readers, he invoked the grace of the Lord Jesus Christ, as well as the love of God, and the fellowship of the Holy Spirit (2 Corinthians 13:14). The Lord Jesus Christ is God in the same sense as the other two persons.

One of the most moving incidents in the Gospels concerns 'doubting Thomas'. On the day that our Lord rose from the dead, he presented himself alive to his frightened disciples, who were met together behind locked doors. But Thomas was absent and simply would not believe them when they later told him, 'We have seen the Lord.' His retort was: 'Unless I see in His hands the print of the nails, and put my finger into the print of the nails, and put my hand into His side, I will not believe' (John 20:25).

John tells us about the events which followed. 'And after eight days His disciples were again inside, and Thomas with them. Jesus came, the doors being shut, and stood in the midst, and said, "Peace to you!" Then He said to Thomas, "Reach your finger here, and look at My hands; and reach your hand here, and put it into My side. Do not be unbelieving, but believing." And Thomas answered and said to Him, "My Lord and my God!"' (John 20:26-28).

Jesus did not reject this astonishing confession from Thomas's lips. He did not say his worship was blasphemous, and that God alone should be worshipped. He accepted it totally. Indeed, he replied, 'Thomas, because you have seen Me, you have believed. Blessed are those who have not seen and yet have believed' (John 20:29). He made it clear that to believe in his deity is to *be* a believer. 'My Lord and my God' remains the adoring confession of true believers today. He is the object of their faith. It is by believing on him that they are saved (Acts 16:31). They know him as 'our great God and Saviour Jesus Christ' (Titus 2:13).

They are not alarmed that the one they adore in this way should have said, 'My Father is greater than I' (John 14:28). Instead, they marvel that the one who is eternally God, and coequal with the Father should have become a Man, and endured such humiliation that he could possibly say such a thing. He was truly a Man, and it was as a Man that he said it. Yet he was a Man who had God as his Father in a unique way. This was because he was truly God. The Trinity is the first great mystery of being, and this is the second. It is a subject which needs a book of its own. Suffice it to say that the true humanity of the Lord Jesus Christ in no way detracts from his true deity. We say it again: 'For in Him dwells all the fulness of the Godhead bodily' (Colossians 2:9).

> Suffice it to say that the true humanity of the Lord Jesus Christ in no way detracts from his true deity.

So where have we reached? We have seen that there is but one God. We have seen that the Father is God. We have seen that the Lord Jesus Christ, the Son, is God. It is clear to us that the two are distinct: the Father is not the Son, and the Son is not the Father. We know for certain that there are not two gods. But there are two who *are* God.

But the word 'Trinity' is not a word of two-ness. It is a word of three-ness, and comes from the Latin word *trinitas* coined by Tertullian of Carthage at the end of the second century. The simple statements of the Bible were being perverted by enemies of the Christian faith and by heretics, and it was essential to have a word which would sum up the great Bible truth that God is One-in-Three and Three-in-One. Theophilus of Antioch had used the Greek word *trias* in this sense in A.D. 180, but Tertullian's new Latin word proved much more satisfactory. 'Trinity' is not, then, a Bible word. But it is used to describe a truth which is plainly taught in the Bible. The Christian church has freely used the word since about A.D. 220. For there are not just two who are God. The Father is God; the Lord Jesus Christ, the Son, is God; but so is the Holy Spirit.

5.
The Holy Spirit is God

A person

There are many people who have the impression that the Holy Spirit is not a person. The title 'Son' which is used of the Lord Jesus Christ immediately suggests personality, but that is not so with the terms 'Holy Spirit' and 'Spirit of God'. The Son of God came among us as a man, but the Holy Spirit has never appeared in so obviously a personal form. It is all too easy to think of him as merely a force or influence that comes from God. And there are passages of Scripture which seem to reinforce this impression: for instance, those which speak of him as a wind, or breath, or in terms of power (Ezekiel 37:1-14 is a good example). But when we look at *all* that the Scriptures say about the Holy Spirit, it becomes clear that he is indeed a person, who is God in the same sense as are the Father and the Son, and yet who is distinct from both of them.

We see him acting as a person. If you simply survey John chapters 14 - 16, you will see Jesus speaking of him as dwelling (14:17); teaching, and bringing things to remembrance (14:26); testifying (15:26); convicting (16:8); guiding, hearing, speaking, showing and glorifying (16:13-14). A mere power or influence cannot do all these things. Elsewhere in the New Testament we read of him teaching (Luke 12:12; 1 Corinthians 2:13); witnessing (Acts 5:32); speaking (Acts 8:29; 28:25; Hebrews 3:7); calling to the ministry (Acts 13:2); sending out (Acts 13:4); forbidding certain actions (Acts 16:6-7); raising from the dead (Romans 8:11); interceding (Romans 8:26); sanctifying (Romans 15:16); revealing, searching, knowing (1 Corinthians 2:10-11); and performing many other actions which can only be done by a person.

Not only does he act as a person, but the characteristics which make up personality are ascribed to him. He is said to have intelligence (John 14:26; 15:26; Romans 8:16); a will (1 Corinthians 12:11); and affections (Isaiah 63:10; Ephesians 4:30). Could Paul talk of 'the love of the Spirit' if the Holy Spirit was just a way of describing a force who is 'God at work' (Romans 15:30)? Could God be said to know the Spirit's mind, if he were not a separate person in the Godhead (Romans 8:27)? And how could men lie to him (Acts 5:3), test him (Acts 5:9), resist him (Acts 7:51), grieve him (Ephesians 4:30), insult him (Hebrews 10:29), blaspheme against him (Matthew 12:31) and call upon him (Ezekiel 37:9), if he were not a person? Who could do these things to an impersonal power?

Could the apostles have said, 'It seemed good to the Holy Spirit, and to us...' (Acts 15:28) if he were a mere force or influence? How could converts be baptized 'in the name of the

Father and of the Son and of the Holy Spirit' (Matthew 28:19), if the first two were persons, and the third was not? Could Jesus be said to have 'returned in the power of the Spirit' (Luke 4:14) if the word 'Spirit' simply means 'power'? The whole point of that verse is that the Spirit and his power are two different things. He *has* power but he is not a power. The same could be said for a number of other verses (like Acts 10:38; Romans 15:13; and 1 Corinthians 2:4) which become meaningless and absurd if you replace the word 'Spirit' with the word 'power'.

The New Testament was written in Greek, and the Greek word for 'Spirit' is *pneuma*. This noun is neuter. This means that the Greeks regarded *pneuma* as neither a 'he', nor a 'she', but an 'it'. Yet in John 16:7, 8, 13-14 etc., Jesus referred to the neuter *pneuma* with a masculine pronoun. In other words, he called him a 'he' when, to obey the rules of grammar, he should have called him an 'it'. In doing so, Jesus stressed to us that the Holy Spirit is a person, and not a thing. At the same time he called the Spirit by the name 'Comforter' (or 'Helper': John 14:16, 26; 15:26; 16:7). This cannot possibly be translated 'comfort', or be regarded as the name for some sort of power or influence. Jesus promised that after his own departure, this Comforter would be to his disciples what he himself was at the time. It is clear that the Holy Spirit must be as much a person as is Jesus himself. It is also clear that Jesus and the Spirit are distinct from one another.

> It is clear that the Holy Spirit must be as much a person as is Jesus himself. It is also clear that Jesus and the Spirit are distinct from one another.

49

A divine person

Jesus is God, and it would be surprising if the person he sent to take his place were anything less. Who could be to his disciples what Jesus himself had been, if he were not also God? And this is the way it was. There is but one Spirit (Ephesians 4:4), and the New Testament gives us four clear lines of thought which display to us that he is God. These are exactly similar to the lines of thought which establish the deity of Christ, but they are no less convincing because of that.

The first is that the names of God are used of the Holy Spirit. He is *called* God. For instance, in Exodus 17:7 we read that 'the children of Israel … tempted the LORD', that is, Jehovah. Psalm 95:8 refers to this incident, and in it God says, 'Do not harden your hearts, as in the rebellion … when your fathers tested Me.' When this passage of the Psalm is quoted in Hebrews 3:7-11, its words are said to be those of the Holy Spirit. In other words, the God who speaks in the Psalm — the Jehovah who was tempted in the wilderness — is none other than the Holy Spirit.

We see the same thing in Isaiah 6:8-9. Here Isaiah hears the voice of Jehovah asking, 'Whom shall I send…?' Shortly afterwards Jehovah commissions him to be a prophet, with the words: 'Go to this people and say…' When Paul quotes these words in Acts 28:25-27, he says that it was the Holy Spirit who was speaking; so the Holy Spirit is Jehovah. He is God. The same lesson can be learned by comparing Jeremiah 31:33 with Hebrews 10:15-16. This is why Peter is so adamant that to lie to the Holy Spirit is to lie to God (Acts 5:3-4). This is why Paul insists that the Spirit of God dwelling in a person makes that person's body the temple of God (1 Corinthians 3:16-17; 6:19).

A second line of argument is that the attributes of God are ascribed to the Holy Spirit. What can be said of God alone, is said of *him*! This could not be so if he were not God himself. A few examples will be sufficient. None but God is eternal; but in Hebrews 9:14 this is said of the Holy Spirit. The Spirit is holy. The Spirit is in all places at all times (Psalm 139:7-10). The Spirit is all-knowing (Isaiah 40:13-14; 1 Corinthians 2:10-11; Romans 11:34). The Spirit is able to do all he pleases (1 Corinthians 12:11; Romans 15:19). These things are only true of God; but they are true of the Spirit. The Holy Spirit is God.

A third line of argument is that the works of God are attributed to the Holy Spirit. Was it not God who created man? Yet Elihu could say, 'The Spirit of God has made me, and the breath of the Almighty gives me life' (Job 33:4). Who but God is able to sustain the universe he created? Who but God is able to work miracles? Who but God can give a sinner a new nature, and make him spiritually alive? Who but God can, and will, raise the dead? And yet all of these things are attributed by the Scriptures to the Holy Spirit (Psalm 104:30 and Job 26:13; Matthew 12:28 and 1 Corinthians 12:9-11; John 3:5-6 and Titus 3:5; Romans 8:11). Who but God himself can do the works of God? But these are precisely the works which the Holy Spirit does!

> Who but God himself can do the works of God? But these are precisely the works which the Holy Spirit does!

In 2 Corinthians 3:18 we are told that the Holy Spirit increasingly transforms the characters of believers. They are changed more and more into God's image. Could anyone less than God do that? In the same way, while Paul tells us that the Scriptures were given by inspiration 'of God' (2 Timothy 3:16), Peter tells us that their true Author is the Holy Spirit (2 Peter 1:21). Indeed, the Holy Spirit *is* God!

A fourth line of argument is that the worship and honour which is to be paid to God alone, is, in the Scriptures, paid to the Holy Spirit. Christian converts are baptized in his name (Matthew 28:19). There is such a thing as blasphemy against him. Blasphemy is insulting the honour of God, and if the Holy Spirit were not God, it would be impossible to blaspheme against him. As it is, this sort of blasphemy is the most serious of all, and can never be forgiven (Matthew 12:31-32). In Romans 1:9 Paul calls on God to bear witness to the truth of what he is saying; but in Romans 9:1, in a similar passage, he declares that it is in the Holy Spirit that his conscience bears witness to the truth of his words. He is not afraid to invoke the Holy Spirit when he prays the blessing of God on those to whom he has been writing (2 Corinthians 13:14).

So the Holy Spirit is called God. He has the attributes of God. He does the works of God. He is invoked and honoured as God. We can only conclude that he *is* God, and that he is God in the same sense as are the Father and the Son.

A distinct person

However, we must be careful to note that the Holy Spirit is a distinct person. He is God, as is the Father. He is God, as is the Son. But he is *not* the Father. He is *not* the Son.

We shall deal with this more thoroughly in our next chapter. Yet the point needs to be established now. Two texts will do. The first is Matthew 12:31-32, to which we recently referred. Here Jesus says that blasphemy may be forgiven. His original hearers would have understood that he was talking about blasphemy against God the Father. He goes on to teach that blasphemy against the Son can also be forgiven. But blasphemy against the Holy Spirit can never be forgiven. It is obvious that blasphemy against the Holy Spirit is not the same act as blasphemy against the Father, or against the Son. For this to be so, the Holy Spirit must be distinct from the Father. He must be distinct from the Son.

The second text is John 15:26, where Jesus speaks of the Comforter or Helper, 'whom I shall send to you from the Father, the Spirit of truth who proceeds from the Father...' It is plain that the Holy Spirit is not the Lord Jesus Christ, for it is Christ who promises to send him. It is equally plain that the Holy Spirit is not the Father, for Christ sends him *from* the Father. Each is God, yet each is distinct. The truth is, as the *Westminster Shorter Catechism* puts it, that 'There are three persons in the Godhead; the Father, the Son, and the Holy Ghost; and these three are one God, the same in substance, equal in power and glory.' That is the doctrine of the Trinity stated in its most simple form.

6.
Three distinct persons

The purpose of this chapter is to emphasize the point which has just been made. The Father is not the Son. The Son is not the Holy Spirit. The Holy Spirit is not the Father. Each is God. Each one is *all* of God. But each is distinct from the other. This truth is not hard to state, but it is totally impossible to understand.

Some people, in trying to make this truth understandable, have merely succeeded in denying it. Usually one of three things has happened.

Some, well aware that the Bible teaches that God is three, have ended up by denying that God is one. They have fallen into the trap of thinking of the three persons as three separate divine beings. In other words, they have become tritheists — those who believe in three gods.

Others, well aware that the Bible teaches that God is one, have denied the deity of the Son, and the deity of the Holy

Spirit. They have refused to accept these two persons as God. This leaves them with but one divine person, who is the only divine Being. Such people are called Unitarians, or Arians.

Others, also aware that the Bible teaches that God is one, have thought of the Father, the Son and the Holy Spirit, as one and the same identical person. There is but one divine Being, who appears at different times in different ways. The names, the Father, the Son and the Holy Spirit, merely describe the different aspects and functions of the one divine person.

If we have grasped and believed the teaching of the previous chapters, the first two of these errors should be no threat to us. We have seen that God is one. We have seen that each of the three persons is God. But while we believe both of these facts, we must continue to stress that the Father, the Son and the Holy Spirit are distinct from each other. This will preserve us from the third error.

The titles, the Father, the Son, the Holy Spirit, are not the names of the same person merely appearing in different forms at different times. They are distinct persons. Hence in John 12:28 the Father says 'I'; in John 17:4 the Son says 'I'; and in Acts 13:2 the Holy Spirit says 'I'. There are three who are God, and each can say 'I'; and none of them says 'we'. But they have in common one infinite intelligence, power and will. So when we say that they are distinct persons, we do not mean that one is as separate from the other as one human person is from every other. They are but one God. To us, their mode of existence in the one substance is a profound mystery. There is no way we can explain it. All that is revealed to us is that the Three are distinct as 'one Spirit ... one Lord ... one God and Father' (Ephesians 4:4-6); 'the same Spirit ... the same Lord

… the same God' (1 Corinthians 12:4-6). They are so very obviously three. And yet it is impossible to forget that they are but one.

We must not believe this simply because it is the historic faith of the Christian church. Second-hand faith is not living faith. We need to see this truth for ourselves in the Bible. Why not look up at least some of the Bible references as we go along? This should be particularly easy over the next few pages, where so many of the references are to the same Bible book — John's Gospel.

The Bible's evidence

We saw in chapter 4 that the Lord Jesus Christ, the Son, is God, and that he is the perfect expression of the Father (John 1:18). But it is also revealed that Christ is sent by the Father (John 5:23-24); came from him (John 16:28); returns to him (John 14:12; 16:28); receives his commandment (John 10:18; 14:31); does his will (John 4:34; 6:38); loves him (John 14:31); is loved by him (John 3:35); addresses prayer to him, using the words 'you' and 'your' as he does so (John 11:41; 17:3; 12:27-28), and speaks of him as 'He', 'Him' and 'Himself' (John 5:19-26). We also read of the Father speaking to the Son, and addressing him as 'You', and

> The Father, the Son, the Holy Spirit, are not the names of the same person merely appearing in different forms at different times. They are distinct persons.

not 'I' (Mark 1:11; Luke 3:22); speaking of him as 'Him' (Mark 9:7); and giving an audible reply to one of his prayers (John 12:27-28). It is plain that the Father is not the Son, and that the Son is not the Father. Their very titles suggest this, but now the truth cannot be missed; and yet each is God, as we have seen.

But that is not all. By reading John 14:16, 26; 15:26; and 16:13-15, we learn something further. The Comforter, the Holy Spirit, is also distinct from the Father, and just as distinct from the Son. Jesus asks the Father to send him. The Father sends him in the Son's name. Jesus himself sends him from the Father. The Spirit glorifies the Son and takes what the Father has given to the Son and shows it to his disciples. We shall look at all these verses again in chapter 8. But at this point we note that each phrase is chosen to make it abundantly clear that the Father, the Son and the Holy Spirit are distinct from each other. One is not the other.

Of course there are other passages where it is plain that God the Father, God the Son and God the Holy Spirit are distinct. Early in the Gospel of Matthew (3:13 - 4:1) we read the account of the baptism of our Lord Jesus Christ. As he comes up out of the water, the Spirit of God descends on him, and at the same time the voice of the Father sounds from heaven, acknowledging him as his beloved Son, in whom he is well pleased. Could there be a clearer indication of the distinction between the persons than this — the Father in heaven, the Son on earth and the Spirit descending?

In the last verses of the same Gospel we read of our Lord's commission to make disciples of all nations, and to baptize the converts 'in the name of the Father and of the Son and of the Holy Spirit' (Matthew 28:19). The use of the word 'and' in this sentence is sufficient to indicate that the Father is not the Son, the Son is not the Holy Spirit and the Holy Spirit is not the Father. And yet the unity of God is not broken: the converts are to be baptized, not in the 'names', but 'in the name'.

We see something similar in 2 Corinthians 13:14, where Paul's benediction is: 'The grace of the Lord Jesus Christ, and the love of God, and the communion of the Holy Spirit be with you all. Amen.' Once more the word 'and' shows that we must regard the Three as distinct from one another. Yet, as we have seen, Paul clearly believed in the unity of God. He invokes all three persons in his benediction, and clearly accepts God's three-ness. He can do this, while still maintaining God's one-ness. We say it again, although the *word* 'Trinity' is not found in the Bible, the *doctrine* of the Trinity is there for all to see.

The word 'person'

But there is another word which we have used a good deal in this book which we have not found in any of the Bible passages we have examined. It is the word 'person'. Something needs to be said about this.

The doctrine of the Trinity is not hard to find in the Bible, but Christians have often found it hard to express. It is not hard to say that there is but one God. It is not hard to say that there are three who are God. The difficulty comes when somebody asks, 'Three *what*?' You cannot say 'three *thirds*', because the Father is not a part of the one God, but the whole of God; and the same is true of the Son and of the Holy Spirit. You cannot say 'three *gods*', because that means that you fall into tritheism, and deny God's unity. So what do you call the Father, the Son and the Holy Spirit? They are the three …? of the Godhead. You cannot go through history leaving a blank. You must fill it in, either by finding a suitable word, or by coining a new one.

A number of different words have been used through the centuries, and all of them have proved inadequate in some way or another. Greek writers generally used the word *hupostasis* ('hypostasis'), while Latin authors used *persona* ('mask', or 'character in a play'), *substantia* ('substance'), and sometimes, especially in the Middle Ages, *subsistentia* ('subsistence'). The use of different words simply underlines the fact that none of them was considered to be really good enough to express what was wanted. Our word 'person' is a take-over of *persona*, and is the word which has come to be used most often in the English-speaking world.

But it is a word which we must use most carefully. We must certainly not use it in its original Latin sense. The three persons of the Godhead are not like an actor in a play, who appears in three different roles or costumes. But nor must we use the word 'person' as we do in ordinary speech. Then we use it of a distinct and individual human being, who has his own self-consciousness — he is conscious of his own separate identity. In God there are not three individuals alongside each other and separate from each other, who, at least in theory, can act against one another. To think like that will bring us back into tritheism. By 'persons' we mean that there are personal self-distinctions within the divine Being, who can use of themselves the word 'I', and of the others the words 'you' and 'he'. But we do not mean that the divine Being is capable of being divided, or is to be thought of as a collection of three separate individuals. Mysteriously, one person can be said to be 'in' another (John 17:21). God is 'one indivisible essence'. In this sense he is one. But this divine essence exists eternally as the Father, the Son and the Holy Spirit. In this sense, God is three. We cannot conceive how three persons can have among them but one intelligence and one will. But it needs to be underlined that we believe it, not because we can grasp or explain it, but because this is what God has revealed about himself in his Word. He is:

The undivided Three,
And the mysterious One.

Once we think of him in any different way, we shall have a view of God which is different from that of the Scriptures. We shall have created a God of our own imagining. This is idolatry.

We are deeply conscious that the Trinity is a mystery beyond our comprehension. The glory of God is incomprehensible. There are no analogies for what we have been describing. There is no way we can picture this truth. You can have three men, each of whom is equally human, and distinct from the other. But at the end of the day you still have three men, and not one. The three persons of the Godhead are each equally God, and

> The three persons of the Godhead are each equally God, and distinct from each other. … [yet] you still have but one God. This God does not exist outside of, or apart from, the three persons.

61

distinct from each other. The mystery is that you still have but one God. This God does not exist outside of, or apart from, the three persons. He has no other existence, except as the three persons of the Trinity. Whatever you can say about God, you can say about each of the persons, for each of them is God, and has equal dignity in the Godhead. In this sense one of them cannot be either over or under the others, and what you can say about one of them, you can say about the other two.

And yet, having said that, there are things which can be said about the Father, which cannot be said about the Son or the Holy Spirit. Similarly, there are things which can be said about the Son alone, and about the Holy Spirit alone. In the words of the *Westminster Larger Catechism*, 'There be three persons in the Godhead, the Father, the Son, and the Holy Ghost; and these three are one true, eternal God, the same in substance, equal in power and glory; although distinguished by their personal properties.' It is to this question of their 'personal properties' that we now come.

7.
The eternal generation of the Son

The title of this chapter may sound complicated, so let us be clear what we are talking about here. We are considering the 'personal properties' of the persons of the Godhead. There are certain things which can be said about each of them, which cannot be said about the other two.

'What are the personal properties of the three persons in the Godhead?' asks the catechism quoted at the end of the last chapter. The answer is simply profound: 'It is proper to the Father to beget the Son, and to the Son to be begotten of the Father, and to the Holy Ghost to proceed from the Father and the Son from all eternity.'

This tells us that if we isolate two issues, we can deal fully with this question of 'personal properties'. We must talk about the Father begetting, and the Son being begotten. We will do that now, in this chapter. Then we must deal with the procession of the Holy Spirit, and we will do that in the chapter that follows.

Son

The key word at this point is the word 'son', and we will be greatly helped if we immediately recognize that the Bible uses this word in a number of different ways. We must, at all costs, avoid the crude notion that because Jesus is called the 'Son of God', this implies that God had a *child*.

Sometimes the word means 'son', pure and simple; but it is also used loosely, in the sense of 'descendant'. The descendants of Israel are thus known as 'the children of Israel' or, as it is in the Hebrew of the Old Testament, 'the sons of Israel'. But very often the word does not carry the idea of 'being born' at all. Zion's citizens are called 'sons of Zion'. The pupils or disciples of the prophets are 'the sons of the prophets' (1 Kings 20:35). Rough and unprincipled people are known as 'children of Belial' (Deuteronomy 13:13, AV), while someone who deserves to die is a 'son of death' (1 Samuel 20:31). These examples are from the Old Testament, but similar uses of the word are found in the New Testament.

We are not surprised, therefore, to find the expression 'sons of God', and do not immediately jump to the conclusion that God has descendants. Earthly rulers are described as 'children of the Most High' (Psalm 82:6), because their power is delegated to them by God, and they exercise it under him. The expression 'sons of God' is used to describe angels (Job 1:6), as well as the men and women who are the special objects of God's love — Christian disciples who have received the privilege of adoption, and are received as members of God's household (Matthew 5:9, 45; Galatians 3:26). But when the title 'sons of God' is used of creatures, whether they be human beings or angels, it is always used in the plural. It is only when it is used of the Lord Jesus Christ, the second person of the Trinity, that it is used in the singular.

The only exception to this is in Luke 3:38, where it is used of Adam. The reason for this is obviously because Adam owed his life directly to God, without the involvement of a human father.

Son of God

But in considering this title 'Son of God' which is used of our Lord Jesus Christ (John 19:7), we must realize that the word 'son' is not used in any of the ways we have so far described. He is not the Son of his Father in the sense that he had a beginning. Nor is the phrase merely an exalted title, like that applied to earthly rulers. Nor is it simply a device to remind us that he became a Man by supernatural means, and not by ordinary generation — though of course it does remind us of that (see Luke 1:35). Nor is it a quaint way of saying that he was nearer to God than anyone else. Its use is altogether different. The first person of the Trinity is called 'Father' to show to us what is his eternal relationship with the Son. The second person of the Trinity is called 'Son' to show us what relationship he in turn has to the first person. 'Father' and 'Son' are everyday titles. But they help to convey to our poor minds something of the relationship which these two persons eternally enjoy between themselves.

The terms suggest and imply that the Son is what he is, because of the Father. But they do not imply that the Father is what *he* is because of the Son. The same idea is suggested by the phrase 'the only begotten' which the Scriptures so often use. He is 'the only begotten of the Father' (John 1:14); 'the only begotten Son' (John 1:18; 3:16); and 'the only begotten Son of God' (John 3:18). The Son owes his generation to the Father, but the same cannot be said the other way round. On two other occasions the term 'firstborn' is used — a term which simply underlines that he was before all creation (Colossians 1:15; Hebrews 1:6). The relationship between the Father and the Son is obviously unique. None the less the Scripture is prepared to help our mortal minds to understand, by speaking of it in terms of generation and birth. It is also said that the Son is the express image of God the Father, and the brightness of his glory (Hebrews 1:3). It would be impossible for him to be what he is without the Father. But God the Father is never said to be the express image of God the Son.

We are not suggesting that the Father *created* the Son. The *Athanasian Creed* is right to declare that 'The Son is from the Father alone, neither made, nor created, but begotten.' The Lord Jesus Christ is not a creature. We saw in chapter 4 that he is God, as the Father is God. Both are God; both are God equally; both are God eternally; and both are God in the same sense. Nor are we saying that God the Father chose to do something, or that something which had not happened came to happen. We are talking about something which takes place naturally in the Godhead, and has always done so — something which is happening now, and has happened eternally. If this were not the case, there would be some change in the Godhead, and that is impossible. Besides, it would contradict the plain biblical teaching that Christ's 'goings forth are from of old, from everlasting' (Micah 5:2; see Matthew 2:6 and John 7:42).

God the Father does not *make* God the Son to be God. He is God in his own right. And yet without God the Father, there would be no person in the Godhead who is God the Son. The Son is what he is because of the Father. Within the Godhead there is something going on which is similar to thinking and speaking. The Son is the expression of the Father. It is for this reason that he is said to be 'the Word', who is with God, and is God, from the beginning (John 1:1-2). This is what the Son is. He could not be this, without God the Father. The Father could not find expression, without God the Son. This is the relationship which the first and second persons of the Trinity have to each other.

Putting this in more technical language, we may again quote Louis Berkhof: 'The following definition may be given of the generation of the Son: it is that eternal and necessary act of the first person in the Trinity, whereby He, within the divine Being, is the ground of a second personal subsistence like His own, and puts this second person in possession of the whole divine essence, without any division, alienation or change' (*Systematic Theology*, p. 94).

> God the Father does not *make* God the Son to be God. He is God in his own right. And yet without God the Father, there would be no person in the Godhead who is God the Son.

The Bible speaks

Scripture after Scripture speaks of the mysterious truth we are discussing. The Lord Jesus Christ is God in his own right; but think of the ways in which he is described. Not only is he the Word of God (John 1:1), and the exact representation of his nature (Hebrews 1:3); but he is also in the form of God (Philippians 2:6), 'the image of the invisible God' (Colossians 1:15; 2 Corinthians 4:4). The main point is constantly pressed upon us. The Son could not be what he is, without God the Father. He is what he is *because* of God the Father.

It is important to emphasize that this relationship of the Son to the Father did not have a beginning. It has always been like this. We must not think that Jesus is only called 'the Son' since his birth as a Man in this world. John 1:14-18 makes it clear that it was his taking flesh that enabled men to see the only begotten of the Father, but he was the only begotten *before* then. He was God's dear Son when he made the universe (Colossians 1:14-20). It was not a status which came later. In the same way both Romans 1:3 and Galatians 4:4 speak of him as being God's Son before they speak of his being born. He was the Son before he came in the likeness of sinful flesh (Romans 8:3). He was the Son of God before God sent him into the world (John 3:16; 1 John 4:9).

Hebrews 1:5-8 is a particularly important passage. As Son, the Lord Jesus Christ is declared to be God, and to reign upon an everlasting throne. It is he who as 'the first begotten' is brought into the world. His Sonship is eternal. This relationship with God the Father had no beginning. It is also unique and beyond our comprehension: 'No one knows the Son except the Father.

Nor does anyone know the Father except the Son, and the one to whom the Son wills to reveal Him' (Matthew 11:27).

In John 5:16-47 Jesus speaks at some length about his unique relationship with God the Father. It is worth having these verses open before you for the next few minutes. The Greek of verse 18 shows that Jesus called God 'his *own* Father' — in other words, God was Father to him in a way in which he was to nobody else. This came across clearly to the Jews who were listening, and they were angered that in this way he made himself equal with God (vv. 17-18). It is striking that Jesus' consciousness of his eternal generation did not lessen his consciousness of being equal with God. Yet he went on to show that although he did the same works as the Father, he was unable to work independently of the Father (vv. 19-24). He could only judge because the Father had committed judgement to him (v. 22). But this did not mean that he was to be treated as inferior to the Father. By no means! Indeed, he was to be given the honour that was given to the Father (v. 23)! If the Son was not honoured in this way, then the Father did not receive the honour due to *him*. So he was aware of his Sonship, and aware that his Father had sent him. Yet, incomprehensibly to our minds, he was aware of his equality and unity with the Father!

As the passage continues, Jesus claims that he has life in himself, as does the Father. Unlike us, he was not made alive by anyone. He is alive in his own right. Even so, he goes on to say that he has life in himself, only because his Father gave him this quality (v. 26)! The divine prerogative of raising the dead also belongs to the Son of God (v. 25); and yet he can do nothing on his own initiative. All the power he exercises

> [Jesus] is God in his own right. But it is clear also that the Son would be *nothing at all* if it were not for God the Father.

is because of his Father who has sent him into the world, and whose will he loves to obey (vv. 30, 36). He comes exercising divine powers (v. 40), and as the subject of the Scriptures (vv. 39, 46), and yet he does not come in his own name, but in his Father's (v. 43). The whole passage shows that Jesus is God, in and of himself. He is God in his own right. But it is clear also that the Son would be *nothing at all* if it were not for God the Father.

A very similar passage is found in John 10:22-42. Once more Jesus speaks of coming in his Father's name, and of the fact that those he has come to save are only his because the Father gave them to him (vv. 25, 29). He is only in the world because the Father sent him (v. 36). That is the language of subordination. It reveals that the Son serves the Father. And yet in the same passage Christ's claims to deity are so obvious that the Jews once more thought of killing him (v. 31). They accused him of claiming to be God (v. 33), and they were not mistaken. That is exactly what Jesus *was* claiming! He claimed he could do what God alone can do — that is, give eternal life (v. 28). He claimed that he, like the Father, could not have snatched from his grasp those whom he had saved (vv. 28-29). He claimed to be the Son of God, who was none the less one with the Father (vv. 36, 30). He did not mean that he was one with his Father in the sense that a son on earth is. Such a person owes all that he is to his father; and so does the Son of God. Such a person is a separate person from his father; and so is the Son of God — in the sense that we are using 'person' in this book. But such a person could never say 'the Father is *in* Me, and I *in* Him' (v. 38). The Son is separate from the Father. The Son is subordinate to the Father, and sent into the world by him. Yet the Son is one with the Father, and is God, as he is. Not only so — but each one is *in* the other. *This* is the mystery of the eternal generation of the Son. It is the mystery of the 'Son of God, begotten of his Father before all worlds, God of God, Light of Light, very God of very God, begotten, not made, being of one substance with the Father' (*The Nicene Creed*).

Problems considered

Now of course this teaching raises many problems in our minds, and we must be honest and say that we cannot answer most of them. We continue to see *what* the Scriptures are saying, but are no nearer to grasping *how* these things can be. How can the Son owe everything that he is to the Father, and yet be God in and of himself? How can the Son owe everything that he is to the Father, and yet not be inferior to him? Human logic can never work this out. All such difficulties cause the unbeliever to mock. He considers such truths to be against reason, and therefore ridiculous. To him they are unbelievable, and he rejects them. In contrast, the believer sees these things to be beyond and above reason, which is a different thing altogether.

But there are some problems which we can clear up, because they arise from individual verses. For instance, Hebrews 1:5 teaches that the following words from Psalm 2:7

refer to our Lord Jesus Christ: 'I will declare the decree: the LORD has said to Me, "You are My Son, today I have begotten You."' This appears to suggest that the Lord Jesus Christ can remember when he became God's Son. If this is so, we can no longer believe in his *eternal* generation. But if Christ is referring back to something which is eternally and continuously true, how else could he have said it? This is certainly what the rest of the Scriptures teach, and we would be wise to interpret this verse in the light of them, rather than the other way round.

In the same way Romans 1:4 and Acts 13:32-33 appear to suggest that Jesus was constituted the Son of God by the resurrection. It is hardly likely that Paul would say this in Romans 1:4, and then go on in Romans 8:3 to teach that he was Son *before* he came in the flesh. We also need to remember Romans 1:3. There Paul talks of Jesus as Son, before he mentions his birth. In verse 4 he is simply saying that the resurrection made his eternal identity clear.

In Acts 13:33, the first time the apostle uses the phrase 'raised up' (the word 'again', AV, is not found in the Greek), he is referring to the raising up of Christ at his birth. When this phrase is used of the resurrection, it is always followed by the phrase 'from the dead', and you can see it used in this way in verse 34. Paul is here preaching that the person who was *born* was the one who is said to be begotten by God. He was not afraid to touch on the great doctrine of the eternal generation of the Son in his gospel preaching!

8.
The eternal procession
of the Holy Spirit

We have seen that the Son of God is what he is, because of the Father. In the same way, the Holy Spirit is what *he* is, because of the Father *and* the Son. The whole picture is ably summarized by the *Westminster Confession*, when it says, 'In the unity of the Godhead there be three persons, of one substance, power and eternity; God the Father, God the Son, and God the Holy Ghost. The Father is of none, neither begotten nor proceeding; the Son is eternally begotten of the Father; the Holy Ghost eternally proceeding from the Father and the Son.' So we see that while our Lord Jesus Christ is spoken of as begotten of God, and we talk of the 'eternal generation of the Son' when we talk of the source of his being, in the case of the Holy Spirit we say that he 'proceeds' (John 15:26), and the term used of the source of his being is 'the eternal procession of the Holy Spirit'. This procession of the Holy Spirit, sometimes called 'spiration', is his personal property. It is the thing which can be said about him which cannot be said about the Father or the Son.

What we are talking about, then, is 'that eternal and necessary act of the first and second persons of the Trinity whereby they, within the divine Being, become the ground of the personal subsistence of the Holy Spirit, and put the third person in possession of the whole divine essence, without any division, alienation or change' (Louis Berkhof, *Systematic Theology*, p. 97).

That is a lot to take in! But it should be clear that we are talking about something very similar to the truth of the last chapter. Similar — but not exactly the same, for there are some important differences. Generation is the work of the Father alone, while spiration is the work of both the Father and the Son. By his eternal generation the Son is enabled to take part in the work of spiration, but the Holy Spirit does not acquire anything similar as a result of his procession. Logically (but not, of course, chronologically — for all that takes place in the Godhead is timeless), generation takes place before spiration. None the less, just as the Son is eternally begotten of the Father, without being inferior to him, so the Holy Spirit eternally proceeds from the

...just as the Son is eternally begotten of the Father, without being inferior to him, so the Holy Spirit eternally proceeds from the Father and the Son without being inferior to them.

Father and the Son without being inferior to them. He is what he is because of them. But he is not God in a lesser sense.

That, simply, is the doctrine of the eternal procession of the Holy Spirit. But how did the church, in the early centuries, arrive at these conclusions? Is this doctrine merely the invention of a few ancient theologians? Certainly not. It is a truth revealed in the Holy Scriptures.

The Holy Spirit

In chapter 5 we saw that the Holy Spirit is a person, who is God himself, and yet who is neither the Father nor the Son. It would be wearying to repeat now everything that was said there, yet the teaching of that chapter needs to be carefully remembered in all that follows. But seeing that God is a Spirit (John 4:24), and all that can be said about God can be said of each of the three persons, why is the third person *alone* called 'the Spirit'? There must be a reason why the name 'the Spirit' is used of him, and not of the Father or the Son. The Father is God, and God is a Spirit. The Son is God, and God is a Spirit. But it is the third person of the Godhead who alone carries the title, 'the Holy Spirit'.

The English word 'spirit' comes from the Latin *spiritus*, which means 'breath', 'wind', 'air', 'life' or 'soul'. This word comes in turn from the verb *spiro*, which means 'to breathe'. The Hebrew and Greek words of the Old and New Testaments, which are translated 'spirit' in our English Bibles, have the same shades of meaning as *spiritus* and *spiro*. The third person of the Trinity is called 'the Spirit' because he is the one who is *breathed out* by the Father and the Son. His unique title indicates what is his relationship to the other two persons of the Trinity. It expresses his personal property. The titles 'the Father' and 'the Son' show what mutual relationships exist between the first and second persons. In the same way the phrases 'the Spirit', 'Spirit of God', 'Spirit of the Son' and 'Spirit who proceeds from the Father' are used of the third person, to indicate what are his eternal personal relationships with the first and second persons. Of course, he is called the *Holy* Spirit because he is the Author of all holiness, purity and beauty, wherever it is found in the universe — a subject which is outside the scope of this book.

The Spirit of the Father and of the Son

In John 15:26 our Lord Jesus Christ says that the Holy Spirit comes from the Father — a truth he had already mentioned in John 14:16-17. He goes on to describe him as 'the Spirit of truth who proceeds from the Father'. This is but one of many references which reveal the relationship of the Spirit to the Father. Addressing Jehovah, the psalmist writes, 'You send forth Your Spirit' (Psalm 104:30). It is because he has this relation to the Father that he is called 'the Spirit of God' (1 Corinthians 2:11); 'the Spirit of the living God' (2 Corinthians 3:3); 'the Spirit of the Lord' (2 Corinthians 3:17); and 'the Spirit of glory and of God' (1 Peter 4:14).

But if we look again at John 15:26, we see that the promise of Jesus is of 'the Helper ... whom *I* shall send to you from the

Father'. What the Scriptures say of the relation of the Spirit to the Father, they also say of the relation of the Spirit to the Son. And so in Acts 16:6-7 modern translations correctly render the Greek 'the Holy Spirit … the Spirit of Jesus'. Elsewhere he is referred to as 'the Spirit of Jesus Christ' (Philippians 1:19), and 'the Spirit of Christ' (1 Peter 1:11).

On a number of occasions it is made clear in the same verse that the Holy Spirit proceeds from the Father and the Son, and acts for them both. Talking of 'the Spirit' in Romans 8:9, Paul switches naturally from the term 'the Spirit of God' to what is obviously a parallel term, 'the Spirit of Christ'. In Galatians 4:6 he insists that 'God has sent forth the Spirit…', but the Spirit of which he is writing is 'the Spirit of His Son'.

But nowhere is this point made more clearly than in our Lord's final discourse to his disciples before his crucifixion. It is true that the Spirit comes from the Father, but only because the Son requests this (John 14:16). When the Father sends him, he sends him in the Son's name (John 14:26). Yet it is also true that the Son himself sends the Spirit (John 16:7), although it is stressed that he sends him from the Father, and that the Spirit proceeds from the Father (John 15:26). With the single exception of this last phrase, 'which proceeds from the Father', the Scriptures say exactly the same things regarding the relation of the Spirit to the Son, as they say regarding the relation of the Spirit to the Father. The Spirit does not send himself. He is 'the Spirit' — the one who is breathed out. And it is from the Father and the Son that he is breathed, so that wherever he works, both the Father and the Son are revealed, and exercise their power (John 16:14-15; 15:26; 14:9).

An ancient argument

One of the most famous councils in early church history was the Council of Nicaea, held in A.D. 325. This council defined the doctrine of the deity of Christ in the most precise manner possible, but was a bit vague in what it had to say about the Holy Spirit. All it did was to declare its belief 'in the Holy Ghost'. But shortly afterwards there arose the heresy of Macedonius, who denied the deity of the Holy Spirit by refusing to accept him as supreme God. To combat this, the Council of Constantinople of A.D. 381 expanded the *Nicene Creed* to read, 'I believe in the Holy Ghost, the Lord and giver of life, who proceedeth from the Father...'

However, this addition did not satisfy everyone. The Latin-speaking churches (known as the Western Church) were anxious to preserve the plain scriptural teaching that the Spirit is as much the Spirit of Christ as of the Father. Mostly because of the influence of Augustine of Hippo, they insisted that the Holy Spirit sustains precisely the same relation to the Son as he does to the Father. Thus in A.D. 569, at the Council of Toledo, they added the single Latin word *Filioque* to the Latin version of the Creed of Constantinople. The sentence we have just quoted was now made to read, 'I believe in the Holy Ghost, the Lord and giver of life, who proceedeth from the Father *and the Son.*'

The Greek-speaking churches (known as the Eastern Church) violently opposed this insertion. At first they were willing to agree to the compromise, '...from the Father *through* the Son', but this was eventually rejected by both sides. The *Nicene Creed* of today is, in fact, the Creed of Constantinople as amended by the Council of Toledo. It is included at the end of this book. It is accepted by the Roman Catholic Church, and by all Protestant denominations. But to this day the Greek Orthodox Church, and other bodies of the Eastern tradition, reject the *Filioque* addition. The controversy continues.

Why do the Eastern churches reject what is so obviously the clear teaching of Scripture? It is because they consider that it makes the Son a second 'Fount of Deity' in addition to the Father. To them, it does not tie up with the truth that there is a subordination of the Son to the Father (a truth we will touch on in our next two chapters). The thought of two who are each a 'Fount of Deity' seems to them to be a threat to the inner harmony of the divine Three. But we have seen again and again that there are truths in the Word of God which human logic can never neatly tie up in its own mind. This is supremely true in everything that relates to the doctrine of the Trinity. The limitations of our minds are not reason enough to reject what God has revealed. Our Lord's language in John 14 - 16 does not suggest, even for a moment, that the inner harmony of the Trinity is marred. The Father sends the Spirit. The Son sends the Spirit. The Father sends the Spirit in response to the Son's request, and sends him in the Son's name. The Son sends the Spirit from the Father. This is the language of unique harmony. It is without analogy. The Spirit is the unifying bond in the Godhead, proceeding alike from the Father and the Son, and is as much the Spirit of Christ as the Spirit of God.

9.
Blessed Trinity!

By the evidence of Scripture, then, we are driven to the doctrine of the Trinity: there is but one God; there are three who are God — the Father, the Son and the Holy Spirit; these three are distinct, and distinguished from each other by their personal properties. Generation is an act of the Father alone. Only the Son can be said to be begotten. Procession can be ascribed only to the Holy Spirit. We have thus been introduced to almost all the chief points of the doctrine of the Trinity. Only a very few points remain for us to clarify, and we come to them now.

The ontological Trinity

More complicated books than this one talk of 'the ontological Trinity' (or sometimes of 'the essential Trinity'). This simply means that *within* the Godhead there is a certain definite order. The Father is first, the Son second, and the Holy Spirit third. This does not mean that one has existed before another, for each person is eternally God. Nor does it mean that one person is senior, the second lesser, and the third junior — for each person is God in his own right, and the persons are equal. It is simply a recognition of the eternal relations which exist between the persons of the Godhead.

The Father is not begotten by any other person. Nor does he proceed from any other person. He is the Father of the Son, whom he has begotten from eternity. The Spirit proceeds from him, and is his Spirit. He sends and operates through both the Son, and the Son and the Holy Spirit, and the reverse is never the case.

The Son is eternally the only-begotten of the Father, and is sent by him and reveals him. He also sends and operates through the Holy Spirit, who is his Spirit, while the reverse is never the case.

The Holy Spirit proceeds eternally from the Father and the Son, and acts for and reveals them both.

Each is equally God, and therefore equal in honour, power and glory. One is not God more than another. None is more wise or more holy than the other persons are. None is subordinate to another — in other words, they do not have different ranks. Yet as far as the personal relations between them are concerned, this definite order exists, and *in this sense*, and in this sense only, a certain subordination is implied. There is a priority, but not a superiority. There is an order in the Godhead, but there are no ranks. When we use the expression 'the ontological Trinity', we are simply calling to mind this fact. This is the way it is within the Godhead. This is the way it is between the persons of the Trinity.

The economic Trinity

These relationships within the Godhead are reflected in the way God *acts*. This is what is meant by the term 'the economic Trinity'. Everything that God does springs *from* the Father. He is first. It comes to pass *through* the Son. He is second. And it is effected *by* the Spirit. He is third. All God's works are works of the three persons jointly. It is true that certain Scripture verses speak of creation as primarily the work of the Father, redemption as the work of the Son and sanctification as the work of the Spirit. But when we look at all that Scripture has to say, we see that in each case it is the Father who is the Cause, the Son who is the Mediator, and the Holy Spirit who is the one who applies and completes.

Of course, we must stress again that the persons of the Trinity are coequal. There is no senior or junior. Yet there is this harmonious order of the persons when the Godhead acts. This is the way God works.

We can see this clearly when we consider God's work of creation. 'In the beginning God created the heavens and the earth' (Genesis 1:1). And yet it was his Son 'through whom … He made the worlds' (Hebrews 1:2). But it is quite

...we see that ... it is the Father who is the Cause, the Son who is the Mediator, and the Holy Spirit who is the one who applies and completes.

clear that it was the Holy Spirit who effected the work (Genesis 1:2), for he is often described as the Agent of creation (Psalm 104:30). God the Father did it, through the Son, by means of the Holy Spirit.

We see it in God's work of salvation. It was God the Father who eternally gave a chosen people to his Son, and sent him into the world to save them (John 6:37-40). It was God the Son who was delivered to death for their offences, and was raised again for their justification (Romans 4:24-25). It is God the Holy Spirit who brings them into the enjoyment and benefit of what Christ has obtained for them (1 Corinthians 2:1-5; 1 Thessalonians 1:5-10). The work of the Holy Spirit follows the work of the Son, just as the work of the Son follows that of the Father. There is not just a certain definite order *within* the Godhead. This is reflected *outwardly* in the way God works. When we use the expression 'the economic Trinity' we are simply calling this truth to mind.

Without analogy

We are no nearer to explaining the incomprehensible mystery of the Trinity, but at least we have been able to survey what the Scriptures actually say about it. The real difficulty lies in understanding how each person can be God himself, and yet stand in the relationship that he does to the other two persons. This difficulty remains, and can never be removed. It is beyond the powers of the human mind to understand it.

However, from the first century and until the present day, a large number of people have tried to discover and use various analogies and illustrations to make the truth of the Trinity understandable (for example — three leaves in a shamrock; mind, emotions and will in one man; the sun, its beams and its heat; etc.). Every one of these has been defective in one way or another. It has either said *less* than what the Bible says, or something *more*, or something *different*. We must face it — the doctrine of the Trinity is without analogy. There is no way *at all* in which we can illustrate it. There is nothing like it anywhere. It is the first and greatest mystery of all. How can a finite illustration ever portray the infinite God? It is the being of God we are considering, and he is, by definition, beyond mortal understanding.

The best way to explain

It is impossible to know the truth about God without studying his Word. It follows that we cannot help people to believe this mystery unless they are willing either to hear the Bible explained, or to open it for themselves. If you get the opportunity to talk about this subject with an enquiring friend, why not, with a Bible open before you, follow the method and order of this book?

If circumstances do not allow a lengthy explanation, we cannot do better than to take our friends to a Scripture verse which we surveyed in chapter 6. At least this will help them to *begin* thinking about the subject. The verse in question is Matthew 28:19, where Jesus commands that we go and make disciples of all nations, 'baptizing them in the name of the Father and of the Son and of the Holy Spirit'. He did not say 'names', but 'name'. This makes it plain that he is referring to but one Being. There is only one God. Nor did he say, 'of the Father, Son and Holy Spirit', as if these were merely three terms with the same meaning, rather like 'I, me and myself'. He is careful to maintain that each has his own identity, and distinguishes between them by saying 'of the Father, *and* of the Son, *and* of the Holy Spirit'. There is only one God. There are three who are God. They are one, in one sense; and three, in an entirely different sense. The Father is first, the Son is second and the Holy Spirit is third. There is, of course, much more to be said — as we have seen. But none the less that, in essence, *is* the doctrine of the Trinity.

10.
Some errors to avoid

We have mentioned that throughout church history many people have attempted to explain the doctrine of the Trinity in a way which is easy to understand. Sometimes they have tried to state it in a way which makes it more easy to believe. But again and again they have not truly represented what the Scriptures actually teach. They have repeatedly ended up with a doctrine of the Trinity which is not the Bible's doctrine.

As we seek to uphold the doctrine of the Trinity in the modern world, the same danger threatens us. Therefore it seems wise to include at this point a brief survey of the main errors into which people have fallen. This means that we ourselves can take the necessary steps to avoid falling into the same traps. Basically, errors have fallen into three main groups. We noted this, in passing, in chapter 6, but will spend more time on it now. Each group is an attack upon one of the basic ingredients of the doctrine of the Trinity, and leads to the truth being compromised, perverted or denied.

Tritheism

This is the failure to hold that there is but one God only. The Jews held tenaciously to the unity of God, and this emphasis was carried over into the Christian church. It has been very rare for those who claim to be Christians to lose sight of this truth. But occasionally tritheists have walked briefly onto the stage of history. Two of the most famous were John Ascusnages of Constantinople, and Philoponus of Alexandria, who lived towards the end of the sixth century. They held that there are three gods, who are all of the same sort, and yet distinct and separate from each other. Greater than their error is that of the modern sect of the Mormons, who do not limit the number to three, and who hold that there are many gods. A belief in many gods is called 'polytheism'.

If we remember and hold to the truth of chapter 2, we shall fall into neither tritheism nor polytheism. And yet it is probably true to say that many Christians, in their heart of hearts, tend to think of God more in terms of his three-ness than his oneness. They think of him more easily as Three than as One-in-Three and Three-in-One. Such people are never likely to become tritheists in the strict sense. But they nurse an error in their hearts which keeps them from thinking of God as they should. This must inevitably mean that their worship of God, and their prayer life, are not what they should be.

Monarchianism

This is the failure to hold that there are three persons who are equally God. In addition to the errors which sprang up in history, there are today a growing number of individuals, movements and cults which are monarchian. They speak of the Son and the Holy Spirit as being God in a lesser sense than the Father. Frequently they speak of the Son and the Holy Spirit as not being God at all! The battles in this area are by no means over! We must insist that the Lord Jesus Christ is God in the same sense as is the Father, and is coequal and coeternal with him. And we must do the same concerning the Holy Spirit.

We first find error in this area in the early second century. At that time there arose the Gnostics, who held that God was one essence, and one person, and that from him emanated lesser divine beings, by which he maintained contact with the world. These are called 'aeons', and Christ was one of the greatest. At the same time there existed the sect of the Ebionites, which declared that Christ was a mere man, and that the Holy Spirit was an impersonal divine influence. The same belief was held by the Socinians who were prominent in Europe during the sixteenth century, and is held by the Unitarians, who continue to the present day. During the last century, when the Bible was being attacked and the miracles denied, the same beliefs found

> **We must insist that the Lord Jesus Christ is God in the same sense as is the Father, and is coequal and coeternal with him.**

their way into almost all of the major denominations. There are still large numbers of 'liberal' or 'modernist' ministers who believe in this way.

One of the greatest threats to the truth about God came in the early fourth century from Arius, a presbyter in Alexandria. He maintained that God was but one eternal person, who, before anything else was made, created in his own image his highest creature. This was his only begotten Son. Arius held that the Son was divine in a secondary sense. But he was not eternally the Son of God, and was certainly not God in the same sense as was the Father. It was by the Son that everything else was made, and it was he who, much later, became a man in the person of Jesus of Nazareth. The first and greatest creature created by the Son of God was the Holy Spirit. He was divine in a lesser sense still.

For a considerable time it looked as if the teachings of Arius would conquer the church worldwide. Athanasius alone stood against him, appealing both to the truths of the Word of God, and the beliefs of the early Christians. Mercifully, truth won the day. Yet Arianism has never died a final death, and has re-emerged in history from time to time. Those who call themselves 'Jehovah's Witnesses' are a modern form of Arian, although, unlike Arius, they do not believe the Holy Spirit to be a divine person in any sense. We must ever be on our guard against the errors which they, and others, are still spreading.

It is unlikely that Arius would have had so much influence if it had not been for Origen (A.D. 185-255). The latter unwittingly prepared the ground for Arianism by one of his ideas which was widely received. He held that the Son was a glorious and divine person, and yet that he was not God in quite the same sense as the Father. The Holy Spirit was God in a lesser sense still. He thus sowed the thought that there were ranks within the Godhead, and this made it easier for Arius to go a step further. This sort of view came later to be known as semi-Arianism, and it was forcefully put forward at the Council of Nicaea by Eusebius of Caesarea and Eusebius of Nicomedia. Some of the semi-Arians agreed with Arius that the Holy Spirit was the first creature of the Son, but a majority held him to be a mere divine energy or influence.

Origen's error, in turn, was probably due in part to the teaching of Tertullian (approximately A.D. 160-240). Although he coined the word 'Trinity', his teaching did not succeed in avoiding the impression that the Son was God in a lesser sense than the Father. His error was very small when compared with what followed. But it shows to us the importance of being exact in what we say on this subject of the Trinity. His error, and the other errors mentioned in this section, can be avoided if we remember and hold to the truths set out in chapters 3-5 and 7-8 of this book. Why not also memorize Colossians 2:9 and Acts 5:3-4?

Modalism

This is the failure to hold that the three persons of the Godhead are distinguished by their personal properties. Even the Arians still kept *some* idea of there being three persons in the Godhead. But sometimes there have arisen those who sacrifice this idea entirely. They are so caught up with the truth that God is one that they fall into the error of denying that there are three distinct persons who are God. According to their view, God is but one person, who, like an actor, plays three different parts. He appears successively as the Father, the Son and the Holy Spirit. While he plays the part of one, the others do not exist. Because God is thought of as merely appearing in different modes, this view is called 'modalism'.

Modalism has arisen in a number of different forms, and appears to have been first held by Praxeas of Asia Minor at the beginning of the third century. But its most famous proponent was Sabellius, a presbyter from Ptolemais, who lived about the middle of the third century. For this reason this error is frequently termed 'Sabellianism'. He held that the one divine person who existed eternally carried the title of God the Father. When he created the universe, and later came among us as a Man, he carried the title of God the Son. And now, when he acts directly in the lives of men and women, he carries the title of God the Holy Spirit. This teaching means that it was actually God the Father who suffered on the cross, and so sometimes Sabellians are also known as 'Patripassians' ('those who teach that the Father suffered').

This error has come to life again several times in the last few centuries, particularly in the writings of various European philosophers who had experienced some sort of Christian influence. It is not very widespread today. But it still exists. For instance, in trying to explain the Trinity to others, Christians often point out that the chemical H_2O can appear as either ice, water or steam. But the illustration perverts the truth. For a start it carries nothing of the truth that God is a personal Spirit. But its most serious error is that it gives the impression that the Trinity is nothing more than the same God merely appearing in three different forms. We said earlier that the Trinity is without analogy, and that we must never try to illustrate it. It must now be plain why this is so.

Sometimes Sabellianism is found in a Christian's prayers. Often he begins by praying to God the Father, but shortly afterwards thanks him for dying for him on the cross. He thus falls into the mistake of saying of the Father what can be said only of the Son. He may then proceed to thank him for his indwelling presence — something which can properly be said only of the Holy Spirit. Fortunately God does not listen to our words, but looks on our hearts, and the mediation of Christ guarantees that our prayers are presented in heaven without fault. And yet it is always dangerous to have wrong views of God, and if such prayers are public they may sometimes be positively harmful to those who hear them. The way to combat Sabellianism is to remember, and hold to, the truths contained in chapters 6 and 10 of this book; and particularly to call to mind the narrative of our Lord's baptism in Matthew 3:13-17, where all three persons of the Godhead are manifested *at the same time.*

11.
A truth to live by

Now that we have the doctrine of the Trinity in our minds, what shall we do with it? Shall we just keep it there, and be content that our thinking has been stretched a little? Or is it intended to make some practical difference to our lives? Yes, indeed. Every doctrine in the Word of God has some practical application. Every truth has some way of working itself out in practice.

A truth to believe

But first of all it needs to be stressed that this doctrine *is* primarily something to be believed. The only true God is the one who has revealed himself in the Scriptures, and *this* is what he has revealed. If we believe something different, then we do not believe in the true God. We are pagans. We worship a god of our own imagining. Tritheists, Arians and Modalists are little different from Muslims or animists. They do not worship the God who has revealed himself. They call on a god who has no real existence. They cannot be classified as Christian believers, and are still lost, and perishing in their sins.

A belief in the Trinity is essential to salvation. This does not mean that a believer must understand all the intricacies of this doctrine as they have been discussed and debated through the centuries. But he must believe that the God who is, is the one revealed in the Holy Scriptures, and that he is one God in three persons. The Scriptures declare that eternal life is to know the true God, and Jesus Christ whom he has sent (John 17:3). They insist that if we do not honour the Son as we honour the Father, then the Father is robbed of his honour (John 5:23). Those who believe in God must have a similar faith in his Son (John 14:1). There can be no salvation to those who have a lower view of Christ than they have of the Father (1 John 2:22-23; 5:20).

So it is that those who become Christian disciples are to be baptized in the name of the Father and of the Son and of the Holy Spirit (Matthew 28:19). Where there is no Trinitarian belief, there can be no discipleship. Wherever there is true discipleship, there is also a commitment to the doctrine of the Trinity.

A truth to love

The doctrine of the Trinity is the foundation upon which every distinctive gospel doctrine rests. While the foundation is secure, the gospel remains intact. History shows that whenever the foundation has been weakened or destroyed, the gospel has quickly fallen to the ground and disappeared. Therefore all who love the gospel, and know its power, love the doctrine of the Trinity, and are anxious to uphold it. They know that the gospel they have is the gospel of *God*. Once it is forgotten who God is, it will be forgotten what his gospel is.

> ...all who love the gospel, and know its power, love the doctrine of the Trinity, and are anxious to uphold it.

The gospel declares that God the Father saves, that God the Son saves and that God the Holy Spirit saves. God the Father saves, because in eternity he chose certain people to receive eternal life through Christ (John 10:28-30), and eventually sent his Son into the world to save them (John 3:16; 1 John 4:14). God the Son saves, because it was he who on the cross bore the punishment of his people (1 Peter 2:24), and is alive for evermore to secure their acceptance in heaven (Hebrews 7:25). God the Holy Spirit saves, because no one can receive spiritual life, and believe and rest upon Christ, until he works in their minds and wills (1 Corinthians 12:3; 2:14; John 3:5-8). The Scriptures constantly show that salvation is the work of the triune God (1 Peter 1:2). When the doctrine of the Trinity is lost or obscured, the same thing happens to the truth about salvation.

Think also about the truths of justification and adoption. There is a God who is angry with us because of our sins. He sent God the Son, conceived by the Holy Spirit, sinlessly to assume human nature, and to keep fully his law on our behalf. Christ, the guiltless, died as our Substitute, bearing the condemnation which our sins deserve, and which God's justice demands. The Holy Spirit brings us to grieve for our sins, and to turn from them. He brings us to rest on what Christ has done for sinners. He brings us into union with Christ, so that his perfect character is reckoned to our account, and our sins are accepted as having been punished when Christ died. God the Father now receives us as his sons and becomes a Father to us. The Lord Jesus Christ stands to us as an elder Brother in God's family. The Holy Spirit is within us, and inwardly assures us that we are the children of God. Each person of the Trinity is involved.

It must therefore be plain that without the doctrine of the Trinity the whole plan of redemption falls to pieces. The doctrines of justification and adoption cease to mean anything. And the same can be said of any other distinctive gospel doctrine. We love the doctrine of the Trinity, because it is the very bedrock upon which our salvation stands. The triune God is the one who has saved us. The triune God is the God whom we love and adore. It would be impossible to love him without loving the truth about him.

> ...without the doctrine of the Trinity the whole plan of redemption falls to pieces.

A truth to live by

May I address a very personal word to you as I bring this short book to a close? There can be no salvation where there is no belief in the Trinity. But this does not mean that wherever there *is* Trinitarian belief those who hold to it are saved. Believing the truth about God is not enough. It is not even enough to recognize that without the doctrine of the Trinity we have no gospel. We must *come* to the triune God. Our sins cry out for everlasting punishment. God commands us to finish with them (Acts 17:30). But we must never think that by our own efforts we can put ourselves right with God (Romans 3:20). How could we ever be good enough for a holy God? But God the Father has sent his Son to be the Saviour of the world (1 John 4:14). It is sinners that he saves (1 Timothy 1:15). He freely invites them to himself (Matthew 11:28-30). All who in true repentance cry, 'God, be merciful to me a sinner,' are received and pardoned (Luke 18:9-14), and enter into eternal life and every blessing that heaven contains (1 John 5:11-12; Ephesians 1:3). None is ever turned away (John 6:37). The fact that you come proves that you are one of those whom God the Father gave to his Son (John 6:37). The fact that you embrace the Saviour, and do not reject him, displays that the Holy Spirit is working in your life (1 Corinthians 2:14). The truth of the Trinity is no longer just a doctrine in your mind. It is a truth that you have come to *live* by!

The truth of the Trinity should lead a Christian to worship. We worship God for what he has done. We worship God for what he has done for *us*. But he has only done what he has done, because he is who he is. To use the complicated expressions of chapter 9, he is the economic Trinity because he is the ontological Trinity. We could never have had any insight into his glory and majesty had he not revealed it. What he has told us is too wonderful to comprehend. It is altogether beyond the powers of our reason to understand it. We could never have discovered it, and we cannot explain it. It escapes us completely. We cannot fathom the mystery. We see that we are only creatures, but he is God. No reaction is appropriate, except to cast ourselves before him, and, humbly, to believe and adore. There is an order in the Godhead, but no ranks. So we adore the Father; we adore the Son; we adore the Holy Spirit. Like the seraphim before his throne, three times we say 'Holy', for he is three. Yet we say 'Holy, holy, holy *is* the LORD of hosts', for he is one (Isaiah 6:3). 'For this is God, our God for ever and ever; He will be our guide, even to death' (Psalm 48:14).

The truth of the Trinity should regulate a Christian's prayers. The Father is first, and prayer should be addressed to him. This is what our Lord Jesus Christ commanded, when he said, 'When you pray, say, "Our Father..."' (Luke 11:2). This is how the apostles prayed. Speaking of his own prayers, Paul writes, 'I bow my knees to the Father of our Lord Jesus Christ...' (Ephesians 3:14); and when they praise God, both Paul and Peter begin, 'Blessed be the God and Father of our Lord Jesus Christ...' (Ephesians 1:3; 1 Peter 1:3). The New Testament knows very little of praying to the Lord Jesus Christ, and nothing at all of the constant repeating of 'Jesus, Jesus' which has become so popular today in some circles.

The Son is second, and reveals the Father (John 1:18). No one can go to the Father direct, for the only approach to him is through the Lord Jesus Christ (John 14:6; 1 Timothy 2:5). This does not mean that we may not address the Father, for we have just learned that this is what we *should* do. But it means that in and of ourselves we have no right to approach God. It is on the basis of who the Son is and what he has done, and on this basis alone, that we expect the Father to hear us (Hebrews 10:19-22). Coming to the Father through Christ is much more than reciting 'through Jesus Christ our Lord' at the end of our prayers. It means that all our confidence that we will be heard rests upon the Son of God.

The Holy Spirit is third. Without him we do not pray, but only say our prayers. Yet often we come to God with heartaches and longings which we cannot express. We do not know what to say or how to say it, but our heart is in our praying. All this is the work of the Holy Spirit (Romans 8:26-27). Whenever we are caught up with Christ, this also is because of the Spirit (John 15:26-27; 16:14). Heart-felt, Christ-centred praying, is 'praying in the Holy Spirit' (Jude 20). If we do not pray like this, we should keep praying for the Holy Spirit's influence until we do (Luke 11:13)!

Last of all, the truth of the Trinity should give us a new reverence for the Holy Scriptures. The light of reason could never have discovered that God is One-in-Three and Three-in-One. Nature does not declare it. Where, and where *alone*, is this incomprehensible mystery revealed? In the Scriptures! How did the Scriptures come to be written? 'Holy men of God spoke as they were moved by the Holy Spirit' (2 Peter 1:21). What is the chief subject of the Scriptures? 'They … testify of Me,' said the Son of God (John 5:39). How can the Scriptures properly be described? 'Every word

> The first and greatest mystery of all is revealed in a God-given, Christ-centred, Spirit-inspired book!

… proceeds from the mouth of God' (Matthew 4:4). The first and greatest mystery of all is revealed in a God-given, Christ-centred, Spirit-inspired book! That book teaches us all that we are to believe concerning God. It reveals what duty God requires of us. It is the Word of the triune God himself.

Let us receive it for what it is, not the word of men, but the Word of God. Let us read it more often, with more care, and with more prayer. And let us live by it. Is there any other way to please him who is revealed in its pages?

Glory be to the Father, and to the Son, and to the Holy Spirit;
As it was in the beginning,
Is now,
And ever shall be:
World without end.
Amen.

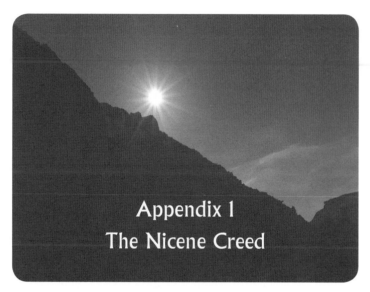

Appendix 1
The Nicene Creed

The oldest and most widely accepted statement of all the points involved in the doctrine of the Trinity is the *Nicene Creed*. This was drawn up by the Council of Nicaea in A.D. 325, and the points relating to the deity and personality of the Holy Spirit were added at the Council of Constantinople in A.D. 381. The *Filioque* clause ('and the Son') was added by a council of the Western Church at Toledo in Spain, in A.D. 569. With the exception of this clause, which the Eastern Church still rejects, the *Nicene Creed* is the creed of the whole Christian church. It reads:

> I believe in one God, the Father Almighty, maker of heaven and earth, and of all things visible and invisible: and in one Lord Jesus Christ, the only begotten Son of God, begotten of his Father before all worlds, God of

God, Light of Light, very God of very God, begotten, not made, being of one substance with the Father; by whom all things were made; who for us men, and for our salvation, came down from heaven, and was incarnate by the Holy Ghost of the virgin Mary, and was made man, and was crucified also for us under Pontius Pilate. He suffered and was buried; and the third day he rose again according to the Scriptures, and ascended into heaven, and sitteth on the right hand of the Father. And he shall come again with glory to judge both the quick and the dead: whose kingdom shall have no end. And I believe in the Holy Ghost, the Lord and giver of life, who proceedeth from the Father and the Son [*Filioque*]; who with the Father and the Son together is worshipped and glorified; who spake by the prophets. And I believe in one catholic and apostolic church; I acknowledge one baptism for the remission of sins; and I look for the resurrection of the dead, and the life of the world to come.

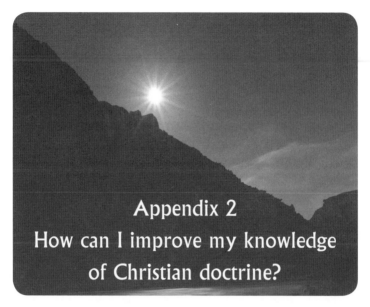

Appendix 2
How can I improve my knowledge
of Christian doctrine?

First of all, start with a skeleton. Then put some flesh on the bones. Then fatten it up. And all the time pray God to send life into it! But remember, a living skeleton is better than a handsome corpse.

Peter Jeffery's *Bitesize theology* (EP Books), subtitled 'an ABC of the Christian faith', gives an outline of key doctrines. It is simply written, and easy to understand, and would be a useful starting point. So would G. I. Williamson's two paperbacks on *The Shorter Catechism* (Presbyterian & Reformed Publishing Company). And I cannot recommend too highly Derek Prime's *Questions on the Christian Faith answered from the Bible* (Kingsway Publications), which I have on my desk, and have used, as I have written each chapter of this book. I would never be without it.

To put a little flesh on the skeleton, next read *The Westminster Confession of Faith* by G. I. Williamson (Presbyterian & Reformed), and that most excellent summary of the Christian faith, *In Understanding be Men*, by T. C. Hammond (Inter-Varsity Press). How I thank God that this book came into my hands almost at the very beginning of my Christian life.

You will then know enough to be able to choose what books will be best for you after that. I must especially recommend *The Confession of Faith* and *Outlines of Theology* by A. A. Hodge; and *Systematic Theology* by Louis Berkhof. All of these are published by the Banner of Truth Trust, and I have used them extensively over the years, and very particularly in the preparation of this little book. I am happy to acknowledge my deep debt to them.

Best of all — join a church where the Bible is explained week by week by a minister who is filled with love for the triune God, and who does all that he can to develop the spiritual life of his congregation!

Index of Scripture references

What the Bible teaches about the Trinity

Psalm 24:3	16	Isaiah 28:23-29	17
Psalm 45:6-7	27, 38	Isaiah 31:2	17
Psalm 48:14	100	Isaiah 40:3	36
Psalm 51:1	16	Isaiah 40:13-14	51
Psalm 51:4	16	Isaiah 40:18	13
Psalm 82:1, 6	22, 64	Isaiah 40:25	16
Psalm 85:12	17	Isaiah 40:28	13
Psalm 86:5	17	Isaiah 44:6	22, 40
Psalm 90:2	13-4	Isaiah 45:5-6	23
Psalm 95:8	50	Isaiah 45:23	41
Psalm 96:13	16	Isaiah 46:10	15
Psalm 97:2	16	Isaiah 48:16-17	27
Psalm 97:7	22	Isaiah 55:8-9	18
Psalm 99:3	16	Isaiah 57:15	14
Psalm 102:24-27	38-9	Isaiah 63:10	48
Psalm 104:24-31	17	Isaiah 63:16	31
Psalm 104:30	51, 76, 84	Isaiah 64:8	31
Psalm 115:3	14	Jeremiah 3:4	31
Psalm 119:68	17	Jeremiah 23:5-6	27
Psalm 135:6	14	Jeremiah 23:24	13
Psalm 139:2-5	14	Jeremiah 31:33	50
Psalm 139:7-10	13, 51	Ezekiel 37:1-14	47
Psalm 145:9	17	Ezekiel 37:9	48
Psalm 145:17	16	Daniel 2:20	17
Psalm 147:5	14	Daniel 2:21	17
Isaiah 6	38	Daniel 4:35	14, 15
Isaiah 6:1-10	39	Hosea 6:3	9
Isaiah 6:3	15, 27, 100	Joel 2:13	16
Isaiah 6:8-9	25, 50	Jonah 4:2	16
Isaiah 7:14	27	Micah 5:2	67
Isaiah 8:13-14	39	Micah 7:18	16
Isaiah 9:1-6	39	Habakkuk 1:12	13
Isaiah 9:6	27	Habakkuk 1:13	16

108

Index of Scripture references

Index of Scripture references

What the Bible teaches about the Trinity